BODY&SOUL

RECLAIMING THE HEIDELBERG CATECHISM

BODY&SOUL

FAITH
ALIVE®
Christian Resources

Grand Rapids, Michigan

Congregational
Ministries
Publishing

Louisville, Kentucky

M. CRAIG BARNES

The Heidelberg Catechism (© 2011, Faith Alive Christian Resources) in this volume is a fresh translation completed by a team of scholars representing the Christian Reformed Church in North America, the Reformed Church in America, and the Presbyterian Church (USA). All rights reserved.

Cover: Dean Heetderks

Co-published with Congregational Ministries Publishing, Presbyterian Church (U.S.A.), Louisville, Ky.

Printed in the United States of America.

ISBN 978-1-59255-745-5

10 9 8 7 6 5 4

FSC
www.fsc.org
MIX
Paper from
responsible sources
FSC® C011935

In memory of the Reverend John Whallon,
my college pastor,
who introduced me to the Reformed tradition.

I rejoice that you are a part of the communion of saints,
because I still need your encouragement.

CONTENTS

INTRODUCTION

I did not grow up with the Heidelberg Catechism. It was not until college that I was introduced to Reformed theology by a local church pastor who was so steeped in this theological tradition that it seeped through every sermon and every conversation we had over coffee in his office. He was the first to introduce me to the catechism's question "What is your only comfort in life and in death?"

I was enthralled with the discoveries about God, the church, and myself that I made during all the cups of coffee the pastor and I downed while talking about Reformed theology. I learned that grace actually precedes faith, that we are providentially held in the hand of God, that our advocate Jesus Christ pleads our cause before his Father, and that the Holy Spirit adopts us into the triune family of God. All of that was life-altering for me. And all of it came from a pastor who had whole sections of the Heidelberg so well memorized that he easily made it a third voice in our conversations.

The first voice in those conversations was always the Bible. The second was the community of faith manifested in a pastor and a parishioner who came in search of truth. The third and cherished voice was this catechism, which never took the place of Scripture but was always present as an honored teacher of the Word of God. That continues to be my understanding of all the church's confessional statements. Through all three voices the Holy Spirit creates a sacred conversation that can reform the church and the people who serve Christ's mission.

Eventually, I knew I had to attend seminary. I wasn't sure then about becoming a pastor, but I was very sure that I wanted to devote my life to these amazing Reformed insights about the Christian faith.

Although I attended a Presbyterian seminary, at that time little mention was made of the Heidelberg Catechism. Perhaps this was appropriate because it was never meant to provide a graduate-level theological education. However, while my seminary equipped me well for ministry in so many ways, what I did not receive was training on how to use catechisms as that third voice that can show up in my work between the sacred text of the Bible and the voice of the contemporary context.

It was not until I was studying church history while working on my Ph.D. that I was able to return to those coffeetime conversations I had with my college pastor about the Heidelberg Catechism. I then gained even more respect for it as I discovered more about the dust and grit issues of the sixteenth-century congregations for whom the catechism was written as a pastoral response. It was also then that I learned it's impossible to understand the Christian faith without the voice of a holy tradition that is always waiting to be our teacher in the faith.

That discovery was about thirty years ago. Since then I have become a pastor and a seminary professor. And over the years this catechism, which turns 450 years old in 2013, has remained by my side in pulpits, classrooms, committee meetings, and pastoral conversations. It is always the helpful and much-needed third voice of tradition that enters every sacred dialogue.

In recent years there has been a renewed interest in catechisms in general, and in the Heidelberg in particular. Perhaps that is because we are finally returning to our tradition to gain insights about contemporary life. And maybe it is also because we live in a day when people are searching for a conversation with someone who can offer a clear and tender presentation on what it means to believe that "I am not my own, but belong—body and soul, in life and in death—to my faithful Savior, Jesus Christ." In the midst of all of the anxieties of contemporary life, no insight could be more comforting.

CHAPTER 1

THE ONLY COMFORT

[HEIDELBERG CATECHISM Q&A 1]

A woman waits in her Grand Cherokee behind a long line of cars caught in construction traffic. She's headed home from her mother's funeral. Her two children sit in the backseat, lost in their electronic games.

Looking around the strangely quiet vehicle, she sees the muddy soccer cleats, discarded Subway wrapper, broken umbrella, and crumpled water bottle littering the floor. Crammed between her driver's seat and the center console is the Vogue magazine she hasn't read. On the dashboard lie the headband she uses for Pilates and the parking ticket she received yesterday when she stopped at the dry cleaners to pick up her dress for the funeral. She smells the dog that isn't even in the car.

Sliding her fingers through her hair, she leans against the car door and recalls the eulogy she just gave. Then she wonders what her children will rise up to say at her own funeral.

A young firefighter finishes his shift and returns to his apartment late in the evening. As always, he's exhausted. He flips through the mail, which includes a notice from the landlord that his rent is going up.

Haunted by how empty the place feels, he runs through his typical responses. He could call the girl he met last Saturday night. Or maybe round up some buddies and go out. He probably should go to the gym for the workout he's postponed too long. Instead he grabs a beer from the fridge and flops in front of the large-screen TV that still isn't paid for. But he doesn't turn it on.

He lies down on the sofa and lets the loneliness wash over him. It's the most courageous thing he's done all day.

A new widower stands before his wife's grave. He wanted to remain there yesterday, after the burial, but his children and friends insisted that he accompany them to the reception. Now he finally has the opportunity to be alone with her.

He's amazed that the world still works so well. The sun came up as always. On his way to the cemetery stoplights changed colors, and he saw two boys riding their bikes over a homemade ramp. How can that be?

As he stares at the freshly tamped dirt, he remembers their plan. They were going to work hard and then retire to enjoy life *together. That was the deal. But she had a heart attack. And now he's alone.*

CONTEMPORARY ANXIETY

I was sitting in the audience for my daughter's graduation from college. The speaker, a well-known politician, launched into the same rhetoric I'd heard at my own graduation. "Your life is in your hands," he said. "You are the master of your own fate. So dream your own dreams, set your goals high, reach for the stars, work hard, and you can be whatever you want to be." Once the clichés get rolling, they're hard to stop.

I doubt any of us are so out of touch with our limitations that we really believe we can be whatever we want to be. We can only be the persons we are—with unique gifts, histories, delightfulness, weaknesses, and besetting sins. Yet the commencement speeches about endless possibilities go down so easily. Just because they're fantasy doesn't mean they lack power.

On the contrary, the power of a fantasy is found in its obstinate refusal to acknowledge the reality we prefer to ignore. We want desperately to believe that with hard work anyone can get the life he or she wants.

This "make a life for yourself" rhetoric is not new. In the ancient myths the quest to get life to the right place drove men and women on heroic journeys through monstrous obstacles. Odysseus's struggle with creatures from the sea and sirens from the shore remains a metaphor for the human struggle against both external and internal forces. Only today we don't confront monsters; we confront choices. Lots of them. Early in life we bask in the freedom of so many choices, but eventually we discover they can create epic levels of anxiety.

When we were children, we learned to choose between good and bad actions. The good was rewarded and the bad punished. As we grew, we connived to get on the choice team or into the most popular social group. Toward the end of high school, we worked out strategies for choosing the best job or college possible. But we weren't just choosing a job or a school or a major. We were choosing a life. We were going to be business owners, electricians, doctors, lawyers, artists, or teachers. If after a couple of years that didn't appear as fulfilling as we'd imagined, we simply switched jobs or majors. The direction of our lives seemed so easy to set, but we could never be certain we had chosen well.

This notion of creating our lives through choices persists into adulthood. We are free to choose a job, a spouse, if and when we will have children, where we will live and how involved we'll be in that community. If we do not find our choices fulfilling, we simply make different choices. And if we don't like the new choices, we need only choose again, and again, driven by the illusion that we can eventually find our way into a life we enjoy. The world stands before us like an à la carte menu: "I'll take one high paying and amazingly fulfilling job, a great looking and empathetic spouse, several close friends, two children, a lovely home—no, not that one. The one over there." If we believe in God, we've reduced the Almighty to a lunch lady who stands behind the counter and dishes up made-to-order lives. The great problem with this fantasy is that it forgets we are mere creatures. Somewhere along the way we begin to think of ourselves as our own creators.

I am both a seminary professor and a pastor of a local congregation. Over the years, in observing the lives of my students and parishioners, I have learned that our greatest danger lies not in making bad choices, but in believing those choices define our lives. Even a good choice can be disastrous if made under the impression that it will save us.

Of course, we all must make choices, hundreds of them every day—from what cereal we'll eat in the morning to how we'll respond to the overwhelming challenges that take us by surprise. God created us with the freedom to make these choices. But none of these choices creates our lives. It's living under the illusion that they do—believing that our lives are only in our own hands—that leaves us constantly anxious and fearful.

Overworked mothers sit behind the steering wheel and wonder if their children will value the sacrifices that have been made for them. What would that even mean? The mommy car, littered with the wrappers of one more meal on the way to piano lessons, one more pair of soccer cleats for growing feet, inevitably reflects the messiness and uncertainty of the family's future.

Young adults who know how to achieve their vocational dreams are less clear about what to do with their loneliness at the end of the day. Even those recently married discover it does little for the empty feeling that emerges when they're exhausted. No amount of success, friendships, electronic distractions, or alcohol can fully anesthetize this familiar, lonely fatigue. In time they learn that the most courageous thing they can do is simply face it.

Older spouses bury their mates and regret the choices they made along the way that prevented them from enjoying each other while they could. If only they knew thirty years ago what they know now, they would have chosen differently. But we are never given such omniscience. So we just do the best we can, which inevitably leaves us torn by regret when our best is not good enough to give us the love we want. And we live in fear of the day, beside a grave, when that becomes all too obvious.

How do we find comfort from such anxiety? Not by making more choices. Our choices lead us only to more doubt and insecurity. They haunt us with the persistent voice that says, "I've could have chosen differently." So we can only choose our way into lives that we'll eventually consider inadequate. That's a shaky foundation for building a life. We need another way.

IS RELIGION THE ANSWER?

Since this is obviously a religious book, you're probably expecting me to demonstrate how my religion provides this better way. I'm on my way to something like that. But first it's necessary to pause and confess that religion has actually contributed to our anxiety.

In our postmodern society we can no longer ignore the reality that there is not one religion, but many. And each offers its unique way of making sense of life from a perspective centered on God. From the beginning of Christianity, apologists have provided rational arguments for why our way is superior to others. But today it's increasingly hard to use rational arguments to prove the superiority of a way of knowing a God who refuses to be confined by rationality. And even if you find the Christian way compelling, the next irresistible question is, Which Christian way? We simply have too many choices.

Most North American churches work hard to develop attractive worship services and programs. That's because, though they rarely admit it, they are competing with the other churches down the street. This does little to relieve anxiety. Instead, it makes people wonder if they're in the right church or whether it's time to move to that popular megachurch in town. We tend to view the abundance of churches as just more à la carte resources. We might choose to be part of one church on Sunday mornings because our family has long belonged, but we participate in another church's Tuesday-morning Bible study, send our children to yet a different church's youth group, or embark on still another church's mission trip to Guatemala. Again, we assume it's up to us to construct a rich life from amid the various resources.

As someone who spends an unforgivable amount of time hanging around churches, I can assure you that religion is not the way to build a fulfilling life. It will keep you busy, but that's just one of its problems. Sometimes when I'm on an airplane and the person next to me discovers my vocation, he or she will launch into complaints about the church. I usually respond by saying, "You don't know the half of it."

Of course, the church is a flawed institution. It's made up of very flawed people. But that's why we're part of it in the first place. To expect any religion to be free of people who have needs and wounds is like going to a hospital and being offended to find sick people.

At its best, the Christian religion witnesses to the way, the truth, and the life (John 14:6). It invites us to settle into a particularly flawed community of faith and allow it to point beyond itself to the God who created our lives and in Jesus Christ was literally dying to love us. Nothing less will suffice.

AN INHERITANCE OF FAITH

Christianity weaves our stories into the much more compelling narrative of God's history of salvation. All week long we are dominated by the problems of our own lives. We're preoccupied with "my health, my kids, my job, and my financial worries." By the end of a week littered with our limitations, we should be ready to come to church and hear about someone who has a better story going than we do. This is what Christian worship offers at its best: the story of God the Father, Son, and Holy Spirit—and now us as well.

In Christian worship we make the bold claim that our lives didn't begin when we were born, graduated, got a job, married, had children or grandchildren. Neither does a disease, divorce, or the death of someone we cannot bear to live without define our lives. According to the Bible our lives start with the words "In the beginning, God created. . . ." The most decisive chapter of our lives is found in the first chapter of John, when the Word "who was with God, and . . . was God" became flesh and dwelled among us. And when we get to the last book of the Bible, we discover that all our life stories end wonderfully—with God wiping away our tears and banishing disease and death. Nothing we can do can change this glorious ending that God has already written for us.

That's why it's a mistake for churches to concentrate on making their worship services relevant to the agenda of the self-constructed life. True worship does not try to cram thousands of years of God's providential work with humanity into individual hearts. Rather, it inserts us into God's history. It catches us up in the great biblical drama of salvation that began long before us and will certainly outlive us.

So instead of constantly striving for what is popular and new, it's appropriate for churches to fill worship services with lots of very old things like Scripture, hymns, and creeds. These things remind us that patriarchs, prophets, apostles, and martyrs have already faced everything that we could possibly face in this life—and they point us to the God in whom those saints trusted. When any of us faces the inevitable storms of life, "my little faith" just won't do. We need the sturdy, deep-rooted faith of that "great cloud of witnesses" (Heb. 12:1) who placed their trust in the God whose story now envelops our own.

Along the stairway in our home hang twenty large black-and-white photographs of our family's ancestors. The photographs date back six generations to the Civil War. Behind each are stories of hard times, war, lost farms, a Great Depression, and loved ones who died too soon. But beneath each of those calamities is also a story of persevering faith. So we call this our "Communion of Saints" wall. As they run up and down the stairs, we want our children to be reminded that they have inherited a great faith. It flows through the veins of their souls. We know that life will not be any easier on the next generation than it was on the previous ones, and when our children encounter hard times we want them to remember that there is more to whom they are than meets the eye. We want them to know that the story of their lives began long before they were born.

For similar reasons the church has long cherished its creeds, confessions, and catechisms. They hang on the walls of our souls as reminders that "my faith" finds its strength as a part of "our great faith."

Creeds, such as the Apostles' Creed or the Nicene Creed, are ancient statements of faith that define the broad ecumenical contours of the Christian faith, the critical beliefs all Christians hold in common. Creeds typically build on the insights of those written previously. And those insights are a vital part of the great faith that holds us today. For example, most churches are guided by the Nicene Creed, which was written in the fourth century and makes clear claims about the divinity of Jesus Christ. All generations need this constant reminder that we have a divine Savior, but we didn't form this idea. It forms us.

Confessions are statements of faith that have emerged out of specific events or struggles through the church's history. Since the context in which we live out our faith keeps changing, confessions carefully express what is at the core of our faith. Catechisms were written with the specific intent of teaching the Christian faith to the young or to those just coming into it. Together our creeds, confessions, and catechisms build a bridge from the Bible to the particular context in which the church finds itself. We gratefully receive these precious documents—written by theologians and tested by synods and councils—as our great inheritance from those believers who have gone before us.

This inheritance belongs to us as a source of strength and encouragement, but in a more profound sense we belong to it as our source of identity.

When we stand in church and recite a creed or even a passage of the Bible, we're doing something that sounds so strange today. We're saying that someone else wrote our beliefs. But can you imagine how awful it would be if we all stood in church to recite our personal mission statements? That wouldn't do much for our anxious souls.

We recite the creeds and confessions as a way of proclaiming that we are part of a great faith that has formed our lives. And that is the way of the Christian religion.

HELP FROM THE SIXTEENTH CENTURY

Zacharias Ursinus (1534 -1583) was a young theology professor. At twenty-eight years old, he had all the right pedigrees from the finest education available at the time.[1] He barely had his books on the shelves of his new office when the German political leader Frederick III summoned him to begin drafting a new theological confession. At first that sounds like a great career move, but it was actually a task filled with peril.

By the time Ursinus came along, the passions of the early Protestant Reformation led by Martin Luther, John Calvin, and Ulrich Zwingli—who "protested" certain practices and teachings of the Roman Catholic Church of that time—had died down. Now the Protestants had fragmented into several theological camps who argued with each other as much as they did with the Catholics.

In this divided Protestant church, Zacharias Ursinus began his academic career. He'd been teaching for just over a year. If he wanted to remain on the prestigious faculty of the University of Heidelberg, he would have to make difficult choices about his loyalties—such was the political reality of the day for scholars. Ursinus had learned that the hard way. He'd been forced to leave his previous teaching position in his hometown of Breaslau, Poland, after being caught on the losing side of a raging theological debate. That experience taught him how easily religion can be reduced to just more competing choices for how to construct a life. But through his diligent studies with the leading diverse Protestant camps, he developed a conviction that all of them held important beliefs in common.

In 1559 Frederick III took over leadership of the province of the Palatinate, in the southern part of Germany. The Palatinate, which encompassed Heidelberg, was divided between strict Lutherans sympathetic to Martin Luther and those Lutherans who preferred the changes Philipp Melanchthon had introduced to the churches. Still others were devoted to the Reformed teachings of John Calvin.

It had long been the assumption of rulers that the people could be held together only with common religious beliefs. (It would be centuries before framers of the U.S. Constitution would begin a "lively experiment" with a disestablished church not under state control.)[2] In Frederick's day people believed that since religious loyalties were of ultimate value, their ruler needed to be able to define and harness these beliefs to keep the people unified and committed to a common purpose.

So Frederick inherited a great problem that created substantial anxiety for him and his people: How could they be held together with their conflicting religious loyalties? Would they be Reformed or Lutheran? And if Lutheran, then what type? If Frederick couldn't resolve this debate, his realm was threatened not only by the disunity within, but by outside forces that sought to exploit it.

Frederick decided to take a huge risk. He called on the relatively inexperienced Zacharias Ursinus to lead a team of scholars and pastors to write a new confessional document, a catechism that would pull together the Lutheran and Reformed churches within his realm. Given his varied theological training, if anyone could understand the nuances between the churches, Ursinus was the man.

Ursinus was assisted in this task by Caspar Olevianus, a twenty-six-year-old pastor who was the son of a baker and who had a passion for reaching out to ordinary people. Olevianus had also been a professor at the University of Heidelberg, but he resigned his position in order to become the minister of a congregation in the city. (His resignation from the university created the opening taken by Ursinus.) Together this professor and pastor, along with a few other local pastors and scholars, began to fulfill Frederick's charge: to write a catechism for the people of the Palatinate. All of them shared a conviction that beneath their differences lay a common gospel of hope.

From the beginning it was clear that the Heidelberg Catechism was developed as a consensus document intended to relieve the anxiety of the people in the Palatinate.[3] Not only were they anxious about their religious divisions, but beneath those pressing concerns lay the more profound anxieties of all humans: What holds life together? How do we know God? What is expected of a life well lived? And what will relieve us of our anxieties?

The authors of the Heidelberg Catechism were not seeking to construct a new church or draft a new theology. Rather, they attempted to dig beneath the particular religious affirmations of the divided churches to find a common faith that provided deep comfort in the grace of God.

A HOLY CONVERSATION

Unlike other confessional documents of the era, which begin with careful theological claims about the doctrine of God, the Heidelberg Catechism begins with the human predicament. Its genius is that, while offering a careful and systematic statement of the Christian faith, it speaks very personally and pastorally to the hearts of anxious people overwhelmed by choices. And that is why this beloved catechism continues to hold such power for contemporary Christians. We still struggle under the tyranny of choosing a life well lived.

The word *catechism* sounds strange and even off-putting. If we have any familiarity with catechisms at all, we tend to think of them as rote memorizations of religious questions and right answers. But that was never their intent. They were written to provide a conversation between the most pressing human anxieties and the biblical story handed down through the centuries. The point is not simply to recite the right answer, but to enter a holy conversation.

The Heidelberg Catechism draws us into a dialogue between our deepest questions and the responses of historic Christianity. It serves not only the church's teaching ministry and its worship of God, but every person in search of relief from the anxieties of the self-constructed life. While teaching us a basic or what C.S. Lewis called a "mere" Christianity, it speaks directly to our deep concerns, addressing them simply, personally, and comfortingly.

MY ONLY COMFORT

The first, and most profound, of the catechism's questions is "What is your only comfort in life and in death?" With almost poetic beauty it sums up the entire catechism by placing us in the embrace of the triune God. Its reference to the boundaries of life and death asks not only how we handle the existential angst of our mortality, but how we deal with all our death-like experiences—such as when a child grows up differently than we planned, a job comes to its end, we lose our health, or our dreams fall apart. These experiences mock our illusions of being in control of life. The catechism begins by echoing our confusion in the face of inevitable losses.

"What is your only comfort?" Notice that the catechism says "your," not "our." This is an intensely personal question—the first of many in the catechism. Every one of us must answer it. Every one of us must confront the reality that comfort will never come by our next choice.

When the catechism speaks of comfort, it's not referring to a sentimental notion that tranquilizes us from life's anxieties. It's not telling us, "There, there now, Dear. It will all be okay."

Rather, the word *comfort* implies a strengthening. (Its Latin root means literally "with strength.") In the words of the Swiss theologian Karl Barth, the catechism shows us how to stand on our feet again.[4] It invites us out of hiding behind our coping devices and calls us to stand again as women and men capable of taking on life with all its volatility.

The comfort the gospel offers is more than consolation or empathy for our worries. It is redemptive. It restores us to our position as humans made in the image of God, crowned with dignity and honor.

In other words, the catechism asks, "What can get us back on our feet as people who are no longer cowed by the next looming loss, the emptiness that re-emerges when we're tired and undefended, or the regret that accompanies most of our choices?" Simply put, "What can make us unafraid?"

I BELONG

The response is startling. The comfort of the gospel is the discovery that our lives do not belong to us.

We were perhaps expecting the catechism to reassure us that God will give us the cosmic boost we need to reach the life of our dreams. Instead, we find that all along we've been striving for a goal we could never attain. It was never up to us to work hard enough to find a life we would want to keep. It was never up to us to hold loved ones close enough to ensure that we would never lose them and be left alone. Each of us can stand only on the affirmation "that I am not my own, but belong—body and soul, in life and in death—to my faithful Savior, Jesus Christ." Those powerful words begin the answer to the catechism's opening question.

Several years ago the congregation I serve buried a beloved couple named Lyle and Sandy. Lyle died first, quite suddenly. A few days after the funeral, when I returned to their home to check on Sandy, she told me about a pair of Lyle's pants she'd just picked up with the dry cleaning. They were his favorite gray slacks. Sandy said that when she saw them she sat on the bed, held them to her breast, and all the grief began to overwhelm her heart. She said she didn't know what else to do, so she began to recite the words of the Apostles' Creed, which she had learned as a child: ". . . I believe in the forgiveness of sin, the resurrection of the body, and the life everlasting." And she said, "I found what I needed." There was no mystical experience, no voice beyond the grave, no light. This was better than that. It was two thousand years of faith holding its arms around her. That alone enabled her to get back on her feet.

The Heidelberg Catechism is less well known than the Apostles' Creed, but it is part of that great tradition of faith that holds on to us and gives us comfort in life and in death. Like the Apostles' Creed, it reminds us that the lives we know, and the loved ones who are so critical to those lives, belong to the God who never loses them.

When Sandy died a year later, I could affirm at her funeral that she was now with her beloved Lyle, who greeted her on heaven's shores beside Jesus Christ. I could say that not just because of what I believe or what she believed, but because of what we believe. We all lose dreams and cherished people, which could make life a continual experience in despair. But if we lean on the great two-thousand-year-old faith of the church, then life is a continual experience of the salvation of God, to whom we belong. In God's hands nothing, and no one, is ever lost. Our only comfort.

According to the early church father Athanasius, Scripture teaches that God created all things *ex nihilo*—"out of nothing." Therefore all things derive their existence from the Creator, even the dust of the ground that God used to create humanity. Apart from the Creator there is only nothingness, or non-being.[5] So when human beings base our identities on anything other than God—a job, being in love, accumulating wealth—it results only in returning to nothing.

When I was a young pastor, I assumed that my parishioners came to worship to struggle over the existential issues of life. But eventually I discovered that was not what was going on in the pews. Mostly what we are thinking about before Sunday morning's call to worship is Athanasius's nothingness. We're wondering how much work we have to get done before Monday morning. We're thinking about the party last night. We're mulling over the hurtful thing someone said in the car on the way to church. And we're wondering what that woman two pews ahead us of was thinking when she bought that dress. We're not really worried about the choices we make that lead us far from our Creator. We're too anesthetized by our favorite distractions for that. Yet some distorted remnant of the holy perseveres in our souls, beckoning us to return to the Source of our lives.

TO MY FAITHFUL SAVIOR

Since we have all wandered into nothingness, God had to do more than throw down a few prescriptions from heaven for how we could find our way back to life. God entered our world and became one of us. That is at the core of the story of Jesus Christ. In Christ, God became human—one of us. This act of self-giving love begins to re-establish the bond between us and the Creator to whom we belong. The marvelous gift of the incarnation is that God comes to our side; God enters our life.

Because God is with us in the human struggle, we are no longer destined to fruitlessly rearrange the circumstances of our lives. We no longer depend on another move, another relationship, or another weight-loss program to rescue us from nothingness, from that persistent ache in the pit of our souls. We can flourish because in Jesus Christ the Creator came to us and restored our dignity as God's children.

We discover to our shame that none of our choices can return us to God and to our God-given identity. On our own we manage only to drag ourselves farther from God. So in Jesus Christ, God did for us what we cannot do for ourselves. He reconciled us to God. He redeemed us from the sins that separated us from God.

Jesus always knew he would be heading to the cross. As the catechism teaches, there he "fully paid for all my sins with his precious blood" (Q&A 1). This Savior who was dying to love us frees us from the "tyranny of the devil," who wants to keep us as anxious captives to guilt.

Whatever one may think of the devil, we can all agree that some force seeks to pull us away from our Creator. Often the pull seems irresistible. But in Jesus Christ, we are no longer powerless to resist it. We have the power to say no. We are no longer compelled to keep choosing things that lead us only deeper into nothingness. We found ourselves in Dante's dark wood because we were not paying attention to the sleepy choices we were making along the path of life.[6] Now we have awakened to the discovery that we have always belonged to a faithful Savior who claims us, both body and soul.

Body and soul. The catechism beckons us to realize that all of life is under the liberating redemption of Jesus Christ. We are free from the despairing notion that our bodies and souls are disconnected. We have long been tempted to think that God may have our souls, but this bodily life is our own responsibility. This makes us suppose that the only point of religion is to take care of our anxieties about what happens after death. In the meantime we are left on our own to do the best we can with our fleeting years on earth. But the work of God in Jesus Christ is so much more than punching our ticket to heaven.

When I realize that I already belong to a "faithful Savior, Jesus Christ," I make the marvelous discovery that he is always at work in all things for "my salvation" in the life I have today. Again, notice that the catechism does not say "our" salvation. Of course, the "our" is implied. But the catechism's authors want us to realize that salvation is not a group plan. It makes its way into every individual's life.

Over the past several decades there has been a lot of helpful, prophetic writing about the dangers of our contemporary hyper-individualism. These days we are tempted to think that "it's all about me"—one more reason we keep thinking of the world around us as nothing but resources for the self-construction of our lives. So it's striking that the authors of this sixteenth-century document use the first-person singular. In their day there was no preoccupation with choices. At that time whole nations would convert to the religion of the prince of their state. But clearly, Ursinus and his colleagues wanted to stress the theological reality that has long existed: if you want to make a choice, choose to believe that your own life has always belonged to a Savior.

Your Savior is at work. As Q&A 1 of the catechism teaches, "not a hair can fall from my head without the will of my Father in heaven." This doesn't mean that God is the one who is plucking the hairs off our scalps or who is responsible for our profound losses in life. It means that God carefully watches over us. But as if that is not comfort enough, the catechism goes on to claim (based on Rom. 8:28) that because God is involved, "all things must work together for my salvation." Nothing is beyond our Savior's capacity to turn evil into good.

These phrases do not mean that everything works out just as we had hoped in this life. Sometimes our loved ones die despite our fervent prayers for their healing. Sometimes we don't get the job we asked God to give us. And sometimes what we were most afraid of happening does happen. What the catechism—and the whole of Christian tradition—means by the claim that "all things must work together for my salvation " is that in all things, both wonderful and horrific, the Holy Spirit is at work, drawing us to Jesus Christ, the Savior to whom we belong.

When a small child skins a knee, he or she runs to a parent. On the parent's lap, the child receives comfort in an embrace of love. Before long the child is no longer thinking about the knee. Love has cast out anxiety. But the comforted child doesn't stay on the parent's lap. We know the child is truly comforted when, strengthened by love, he or she jumps off, ready to embark on the next adventure.

Jesus Christ gets us back into the lap of our heavenly Father and, consequently, back on our feet as people confident in the knowledge of who and whose we are.

After his death and resurrection, our Savior ascended into heaven to sit at the right hand of his Father. But Jesus' work is not done. He continues to unfold his salvation in our lives through the Holy Spirit. This is what Q&A 1 means by stating that "Christ, by his Holy Spirit, assures me of eternal life." The Spirit offers this assurance by working through all things to bind us to Jesus. As we get glimpses of this, it overhauls our perspective of life. More and more we begin to see our lives revolve around God and what God is doing. We begin to escape the claustrophobic confines of our little world. As the catechism puts it, the Spirit "makes me wholeheartedly willing and ready from now on to live for [Christ]."

Thus we find comfort for our weary and often anxious souls not by eventually choosing our way into the life of our dreams and not by celestial protection from skinned knees and broken hearts. Nor does our comfort come from a theology about Jesus Christ. We find our comfort *in* Jesus Christ.

The catechism teaches each of us to claim that my only comfort is "that I am not my own, but belong—body and soul, in life and in death—to my faithful Savior, Jesus Christ." It is Jesus who brings us back into the embracing arms of Father, Son, and Holy Spirit. The great tradition of Christianity has always confessed this as the only comfort that can get us back on our feet today and give us hope for tomorrow and all eternity.

CHAPTER 2

OUR MISERY AND OUR MEDIATOR

(Q&A 2-25)

A ninety-year-old man sits in his small room in the assisted living wing of the Ten Oaks Retirement Center. It's a nicely appointed facility with hunter green carpet, dark-stained doors, and a lobby that looks like the Marriott. Prints of seashores adorn the walls. It's a lovely place, but it doesn't look like home. And behind the residents' doors life is not so elegant. The old man's room has a bed, a sink, a chair with frayed arms from home, a dresser bearing family photographs, and an oxygen tank. A television is perched on the wall. This is now his world.

Every day he remembers the days he wasted. There was always another report to write, another deal to make, another rung of the ladder to climb at work. He thinks about the piano recitals he missed, the soccer games he only heard about where his daughter scored the winning goal, and the wife he loved who died too soon. He used to tell himself that he was working so hard in order to be a good provider, but he doesn't buy that anymore.

*These days he lives mostly with regret about missed opportuni-
ties. But now that he is at last void of distractions, he has learned
to pray again. He prays mostly for the children he dearly loves
who learned from him how to work too hard.*

*He is waiting for a visit from the young pastor who recently
came to the church he used to attend with his family. The old
man is no longer able to go to the worship services, which he
considers a pity because now he's now ready to engage in serious
worship.*

*The pastor rushes into the room thirty minutes late with a
little communion kit tucked under his arm. Apologizing, he sits
down and begins unpacking the sacrament while offering a few
platitudes about how important the old man still is to the congregation. He then launches into the "Liturgy for In-Home Communion." The old man's hand shakes as he takes the little broken
wafer called "the Body of Christ." He doesn't really understand
all the theology of this ritual, but he does know it means he is
somehow forgiven. He receives the grace between yellowed teeth
and says, "Amen."*

*When they finish the old man tries to express his gratitude,
but to his embarrassment he begins to cry.*

*For the first time in his frantic day, the young pastor stops.
He plops back down in the chair next to the old man's bed, finally
catching the holiness of this moment. This elderly man has been
forced to give up most everything his pastor still has for now—
home, health, family, job, and future. The one with all the losses
is thankful, while his pastor is rushing around, trying to accom-*

plish more. He holds the old man's spotted hand, and the two of them sit in silence.

On the drive home, it occurs to the young pastor that he can't remember the last time he prayed in an unofficial capacity.

WHO'S ASKING?

Nobody plans on ending life with regret. But at the end we discover that life sped past us so quickly—while we were just trying to keep our heads above water—that the really big questions got short shrift. The Heidelberg Catechism tries to break into this hurried cycle. It does so by confronting us with the most serious questions of all. Those questions are not about where we will work, how we will achieve our dreams, who or if we will marry, or how we will cope with life's challenges. Those are all important. But they distract us from the deeper, penetrating questions of the soul that determine whether our lives end in regret or doxology.

Our response to a question depends on the questioner. When the cashier at the grocery store asks, "How are you?" you know she isn't interested in a serious response. So you just say, "Fine," hand her your money, and keep moving. She's just being polite. And it isn't polite for you to hold up the line behind you by telling her about your arthritis. But when people who love you place both hands on your shoulders, look you in the eyes, and slowly ask the same question, you know they want the truth. The last thing they're looking for is a polite response.

"What is your only comfort in life and in death?" That haunting first question of the catechism echoes down through the centuries. But whose voice does it echo? Is this just another theological question Christians have long asked each other—one to which we respond with polite piety, "Jesus," then keep moving? Certainly not. If we're just talking to ourselves, we've limited theology to human "wishes and yearnings projected into heaven." We've reduced faith to longings, and spirituality to correct religious answers.

Theologian Eberhard Busch claims there is no object or divine person at the center of these human questions—just a desire for one. We're not having a conversation with God, but one that is merely about God. At its best, such theology can only reveal our common human yearning for comfort. And we can only imagine that Jesus provides it because some other humans suggested the idea.

But what if God is the one who is asking us, "What is your only comfort?" That changes everything. What if the only one who can provide true comfort has just grabbed you by the shoulders, looked deep into your soul, and asked, "How are you?" No one can offer a glib "Fine" and keep moving. Suddenly all of our hustling about to make life right is stopped dead in its tracks. We're forced to tell God the truth. *This* is the real function of theology, catechisms, and confessional statements. They nurture conversations not just between humans or even between individuals and the great tradition of faith that precedes us. They begin an intimate, holy dialogue between us and our Comforter, between us and our God.

True spirituality starts not with humanity's yearning for something to salve our anxiety, but with the God who questions us. And there is nothing polite about this conversation.

"What is your only hope?" God's question rips away all the responses we've learned over the years. We can no longer say, "Well, at least I can work hard" or "I'm a real good mother" or "As long as I have my health. . . ." When God interrogates us, we realize how inadequate all our responses sound. Nothing but the truth can flow from our lips. Nothing we hold and nothing we do have relieved the deep anxieties that lie just beneath the surface of what only appears to be a comfortable life.

In this holy conversation, God not only asks the questions but also presses us to face an intensely personal dilemma. And the dilemma is that everything we have done in reaction to fear and anxiety has pushed us farther away from God. The Bible calls this sin.

We fret about losing the job in which we strive so hard to find security. Our children give us almost daily opportunities to realize how inadequate we are as parents. And we know we'll eventually lose our health. We don't think of our responses to these things as sin. We're just doing our best amid the unavoidable limitations of life. But sin is anything that separates us from God. And a sure sign of that separation is our constant search for something other than God to comfort our anxious souls. By graciously and relentlessly asking us, "What is your only comfort?" God reveals that everything and everyone else to whom we have looked for comfort has only driven us farther from it. That is the sin and alienation of the lost child of God.

A young woman sits in her elegantly appointed law office, long after most everyone else has gone home. She is staying late not because she loves her work, but because she is hoping one of the firm's partners will notice. It's now quiet enough for her to hear the hum of the florescent lights above her. When the janitor comes to collect her trash, she chats with him awhile and is sad when he has to move along. It occurs to her that this conversation has been the highlight of her day. She stares again at her computer screen, at the brief she is trying to write. But she sees only more unimportant words about an issue unimportant to her, which may be read by people who will not place any great importance on it.

Alone in the office she begins to wonder why she works so hard for a life that seems so unimportant, even to her. Her friends are having drinks at a nearby watering hole, but she declined the invitation to join them because she has grown to hate that scene almost as much as her work. She knows that tonight will be like most of the others. She'll stay at work a while longer and knock out this legal brief. No one will notice. Then she'll drive home in her BMW to her high-rise apartment, heat up the leftovers she took home after a bad date, watch a little late-night TV, and hope she can fall asleep.

Another woman is finishing up her workday at the plant where she watches over a machine that pumps soft drinks into bottles. It could easily be mindless work, but she has never allowed that. Of course, she would rather have a high-paying job with a comfortable office somewhere, but the opportunities of life never gave her the education she would need for such a job. She doesn't spend a lot of time thinking about that, though. She's grateful to be working at all. When her friends at work have problems, she's always the person they ask to talk to. And she knows that this is the real reason she is at the plant.

As she shuts down the bottling machine, she takes a moment to finger the cross that hangs around her neck. She wipes her hands on her apron as she takes it off. Then she heads to her car and drives to the homeless shelter where she joins friends from her church. Before long she is placing canned stew over a plate of rice. She hands it to a man with too many wrinkles on his face, smiles, and says, "God bless you."

SIN AS MISERY

Q&A 2-11 of the Heidelberg Catechism confront us with the debilitating problem of sin. (Interestingly, this is the catechism's shortest section.) True to its pastoral nature, the catechism begins by reminding us that we confess our sin not to wallow in our guilt, but only to discover the comfort of how we are set free from it.

To sin is not just to do something wrong. It is to surrender to a power that pulls us from God. Like slaves or addicts we may yearn for freedom. But we are incapable of finding freedom from the tyranny of sin on our own. Trying harder is useless. It's only as we surrender to this harsh indictment that God's liberation in Jesus Christ flows into our souls like a river of grace. Yet we cannot find the courage to confess our sin without first hearing the good news that forgiveness and freedom are possible. This is why the catechism proclaims freedom before it delves into the depths of our enslaved, sinful condition apart from God. Once we discover the holy comfort of our salvation, we can then spend life as an expression of thankfulness to God for it.

This process of confession—finding freedom from sin, then living a life of gratitude (Q&A 2)—provides the outline for the rest of the catechism.

As the catechism starts probing the destructive power of sin, what's striking is that it describes sin not merely as breaking God's law, failing to do right, hurting others, or serving idols. The framers of the catechism would certainly agree that sin is all of that. Their deepest interest, however, is in the effect of sin: it makes us miserable.

Sin separates us from the joy and comfort of being in communion with God. *Communion with God*—that's a term we don't readily use. It sounds like an extra-sensory gift reserved for saints and mystics. But the biblical story tells us that we were all created for a loving relationship with God. And regardless of the circumstances of life, we are only fully alive when we are attending to this relationship. This is why we pray, read the Bible devotionally, worship, participate in a spiritual community, and engage in God's mission in the world. We do these things for the same reason that people in love spend time with each other—they help us grow closer to our holy Lover. Sin is anything we do that distracts us from this communion. And the result is always the same: we are as miserable as lovers always are when their relationship is on the rocks.

A couple of pages back you read the stories of two very different women in very different jobs. One is miserable while the other abounds in hope and joy. What makes the difference? Clearly not the prestige of their jobs. No, the only difference is that the woman at the plant is in communion with her Creator. Her circumstances cannot define her. Instead she knows her identity as the beloved daughter of a heavenly Father. She knows that God watches over every monotonous moment of her work, piercing it with opportunities to say things of eternal value to those around her. The other woman has ignored her birthright. She has given her soul to a job that can never love her.

If you ask the miserable woman in the law office if she would be willing to change places with the joyful woman in the bottling plant, the chances are great that she would say, "Well, no. I don't think so." That's because the addictive power of sin has pulled her far from the delight we find only in communion with God, a delight that does not depend on our circumstances.

Augustine ran into a similar situation long before he became a saint, while he was still searching for deliverance from his despair. He was on his way to present a lecture filled with lies that would flatter the emperor. And he was miserable about it, as he was about his whole life. Along the way he saw a beggar who was filled with joy. But he knew that even though the beggar had what he so desperately wanted, he could never find the courage to trade lives with him. He was too comfortable in his misery, too far entwined in the power of sin. Augustine knew he was addicted to a life that could not make him rejoice.

This is what the Bible is trying to get at when it talks about sin. It is not just concerned with the rules we break or the mistakes we make as we stumble through life. For this reason the catechism doesn't speak about *sins*, but *sin*. It focuses on the condition of misery that smothers us when we place something or someone else as the god of our lives.

The doctrine of original sin describes how we are all sinful from the start. But the catechism goes deeper. It describes our original goodness:

> God created [people] good and in his own image,
> that is, in true righteousness and holiness,
> so that they might
> truly know God their creator,
> love him with all their heart,
> and live with God in eternal happiness,
> to praise and glorify him. (Q&A 6)

We were created for the high purpose of knowing God intimately. Think of God walking in the Garden of Eden with Adam and Eve in the "cool of the day." As the twentieth-century Orthodox priest and theologian Alexander Schmemann taught, we were given the fruit of the garden to eat with a grateful heart, which means that all of life was originally an experience of holiness. Our original sin was to take the fruit simply because we desired it—not as an expression of gratitude to our Creator. Ever since, we've been trying to recreate life's garden in our own image of goodness. We've become stuck with ourselves as gods and lost fellowship with our loving Creator. And we are no good at being gods. So our re-creation strategies result only in the loss of our holiness, joy, and delight. Then God comes looking for us. And God finds us hiding deep in the bushes of our misery (Gen. 3:1-10).

I have been a pastor long enough to know that just because people are miserable, that does not mean they want to change. They may change their jobs, move to a new town, buy another car, or find another relationship, but essentially they're just rearranging the furniture of their lives. What they really need is a new life. They need to stop thinking about their next plan for achieving a life and begin to ponder what it means to receive the life God gives them. In other words, they need to give up control. But that is too frightening for most of us to consider. In my experience people prefer the misery they know to the mystery they do not. And nothing is more sinful than settling into comfortable misery.

THE MEASURE OF OUR MISERY

Years ago one of my sons had a dangerously high fever. So we took him to the emergency room, where doctors quickly got the fever under control. But we wouldn't have known about the danger he was in without a thermometer. That's like the grace of God's law. As the catechism teaches, the law is how we come to know our misery (Q&A 3). It's a grace because when everyone is running the same high fever, it's easy to think that's normal. But it's not normal. Or at least it shouldn't be normal. We care about the law because it reveals the sin that is a fever to our souls.

Today those of us in Western society have grown so accustomed to misery and despair that we think it's the norm. A generation ago, when I was a boy looking at the Sears and Roebuck catalogue, the models all smiled, as if to say that if you buy their clothes you'll be as happy as they appear. As silly as this marketing ploy was, it at least assumed happiness was something we all desired. But today's fashion models often appear sad or sullen, even emaciated. Now the message seems to be, "Buy our jeans because we understand how sad you are. That's okay because despair is cool." People don't buy into this media image just because it's fashionable. Despair has become our standard for evaluating style because so many of us are drowning in it.

True, some people today remain devoted to the elusive pursuit of happiness—so much so that they reject any laws, standards, or judgments against them. They believe that freedom means being able to search for happiness wherever it may lie. But the relentless nature of their search reveals its futility.

They keep moving from one relationship, job, or daring experience to the next, but they never find anything that can satisfy their insatiable thirst. The self-directed pursuit of happiness is a merciless and elusive god. It is as enslaving as despair.

Recently some psychotherapists have noted a disturbing trend among the twenty-somethings who come to them seeking help. These young adults were raised by baby boomers who felt too pressured to achieve when they were growing up. So the baby boomers resolved that when it came to their own kids, they just wanted them to be happy. And now we have raised a generation for whom happiness has been the goal. When they were children, everyone got a trophy regardless of how well they did in competition. When their school assignments became too challenging, their parents rushed to complain to the teachers. When they decided on a whim that they wanted to play guitar, their parents bought the best one they could find, signed them up with the best teacher in town, and didn't complain when the kids decided to drop the whole thing. Their houses were made child-safe, their car seats sturdy enough to handle re-entry from the moon. Many of them grew up thinking supervised play dates had always been the norm. Parents worked hard to ensure their children would never get hurt.

Now some of these young adults are surprised when they cannot get a good job or have to move back into their parents' home after college. But what surprises the therapists is that those who *do* have great jobs, cool cars, and their own apartments are the ones coming in for therapy. They begin by lamenting, "I'm not happy." After the therapist pokes around a bit, revealing how wonderful their lives actually are, the young adults say, "Well, I guess I am happy. But I could be happier." Right. Of course, we could always be happier.

The conclusion these therapists are making is that happiness can never be a worthy goal. Parents need to give their children higher aspirations.

Some of our worst mistakes in life begin as an effort to make ourselves happy. The catechism reminds us that this is our inherited nature, and it's as old as Adam and Eve (Q&A 7). According to the biblical story of creation, we were placed in a garden in which we did not have everything. In the middle of the Garden of Eden was a tree with forbidden fruit, the "tree of the knowledge of good and evil." And every day Adam and Eve had to walk by this tree and remember that they were never created to have it all. That is God's idea of paradise.

Each of us is also created to live a life in which something will always be missing. This is simply the nature of being a creature rather than the Creator, who alone is whole and complete and lacking in nothing. But the holes in our little piece of paradise can drive us wild with anxiety. So rather than enjoy the blessings of the many fruits we are given, we become obsessed about what we don't have. We're tempted to reach beyond our created limitations to grab for it, and that's when we do an extraordinary amount of damage to our lives. It is then we discover that the life God gave us really was paradise. Only now it is paradise lost.

For example, a woman flies into a city and rushes to the hospital to visit her dying mother, who lies in a coma. Things have not been good between them over the years. Because they each had such different ideas about what happiness looks like, they were a constant source of disappointment to each other. Now as she sits by the bed, the daughter remembers all the times her mother asked her to visit so they could make things better. She would give anything for a chance to tell her mother that she loves her. She curses herself and tries to say the tender words that will never be heard. But she's too late. Chasing an elusive happiness her whole life, the daughter lost the created relationship she was given to enjoy with her mom. Of course, there were limits to that relationship, but only after it is over does she realize it was actually paradise.

The law simply reveals the misery of our broken boundaries. Not only did we lose the paradise of our relationships with each other, as the naked shame of Adam and Eve symbolizes in that primal story. We also found ourselves hiding from the One who created us and loves us. This is not just a contemporary problem. As answer 9 of the catechism reminds us, from very near the beginning it has been our nature to rob ourselves of the Creator's gifts. The law is the thermometer that depicts the fever now burning hot in our souls.

Some Christians assume the Old Testament law is an ancient code of behavior no longer applicable to those on this side of Jesus' saving work. We believe Jesus saved us from worrying about standards we could never meet anyway. So we're off the hook. But it was never Jesus' mission to get rid of the law. Instead, he was devoted to fulfilling it (Matt. 5:17-29).

That's why at this point, instead of reciting the Ten Commandments, the catechism focuses on Jesus' summary claim that all God ever wanted was for us to love him with all of our hearts, souls, and minds, and to love our neighbor as ourselves (Q&A 4; Matt. 22:37-40). But if we ponder this summary of the law, it soon becomes clear that Jesus was not getting us off the hook for having to follow the law. Instead, he was demonstrating how completely we are judged by it. We are shocked by the catechism's striking claim that "I have a natural tendency to hate God and my neighbor" (Q&A 5). We might agree that none of us loves either God or our neighbor sufficiently. But hate them? The point is that we always tend to place ourselves first, before God and our neighbor, and that defines our miserable lovelessnes. Therefore, we don't even know how to love ourselves, since the most loveable thing about a life is devotion to God and neighbor. Apart from this, no matter how successful or careful we may be, life is always a misery.

The catechism makes it clear that sin has consequences. And they're severe. By all rights, the misery we feel during our earthly sojourn should be an eternal experience of hell. Hell is where we get what we always wanted in our sin: separation from God. Some parts of the Bible—and much of medieval Christian literature—are filled with horrific images of hell as a place of fire and torment. But for creatures who were created to enjoy holiness, nothing could be more tormenting than to be separated from God now and in eternity.

God is merciful and forgiving of our sins, but we cannot understand God's mercy apart from God's justice. God insists that we be what he created us to be as his image-bearers. The fundamental fracture of our relationship requires atonement and reconciliation. To atone for sin is to do what is necessary to make things right again. Even if we could somehow make up for the righteous laws we have broken, which we cannot, what could we possibly do to atone for breaking the heart of God by our sin? Not only can we not make the payment for the claims of justice, we only "increase our debt every day" (Q&A 13). As David illustrates after his sin with Bathsheba (2 Sam. 11), the only way we know how to manage sin is with more sin. So how do we find our way back home to God?

For the past two thousand years theologians have offered different ways of understanding atonement. Some have stressed the need for Jesus Christ to die to pay the just penalty for our sins. Others have focused more on God taking on our misery and brokenness through the incarnation and the cross. What all theologies of the atonement have in common is our need for a Savior, and only the just God can provide such mercy. We have no hope of regaining paradise and reconciled, holy relationships by working hard or by gaining spiritual insight. Hope comes not from our moral climb up to God, but from God climbing down to us. So now the Heidelberg Catechism is ready to introduce Jesus Christ.

OUR MEDIATOR

The catechism introduces the person and work of Jesus Christ by calling him a mediator. Typically when we think about mediators, we think of a neutral party who stands between two other parties who are in conflict. The neutral party struggles to provide a compromise resolution. This is not what the catechism means.

Our mediator cannot try to talk God into compromises on righteousness. Our sin is simply too much for such an effort. God created us "in true righteousness and holiness" so that we might live in communion with him (Q&A 6). When we compromised the holiness we were created to bear, we lost God. Since salvation means having our relationship with God restored, it can never be found by easing up on the expectations of our created identity as holy and righteous. So there is no deal to be made.

Medieval monks tried to offer penance for the sins of the world. They spent their lives praying for the world's redemption. But as St. Anselm finally made clear, all humans are sinful, and no sinful human can atone or be the mediator for the sin of others. The catechism echoes this when it claims "no mere creature can bear the weight of God's eternal wrath against sin and deliver others from it" (Q&A 14).

We lose fellowship with God as a result of our sin. But the deeper truth is that we sin in order to lose fellowship with God. When Adam and Eve reached for the forbidden fruit, it was because they believed what the serpent told them—that by eating it they would become like God. As the catechism reminds us, we have inherited this corrupt nature to do whatever is necessary to be our own gods (Q&A 7). This is the source of God's wrath. God is not furious that we broke some rule, but that we broke THE fundamental rule: that God alone is God, and we are not.

Wrath is a word that terrifies us when applied to God. It is a much weightier and more righteous word than *anger*. I have a hard time getting through a day if my wife is angry at me for forgetting to take out the garbage. So how do I possibly live in awareness of the wrath of a Divine Lover whom I have scorned by everything I've done to separate myself from holiness?

Ironically, the only hope I have is that it is God's heart I have broken—and that it is God who is my judge. Here's how the psalmist makes that startling claim: "If you, LORD, kept a record of sins, LORD, who could stand? But with you there is forgiveness, so that we can, with reverence, serve you" (Ps. 130:3-4).

God's wrath is so weighty that we cannot begin to carry it on our own. We need a Savior who has the capacity to bear our sin and make us holy again. The only way we can be saved is through a holy human being who can atone for our sin. This Savior must be human to bear the judgment against us that God's justice demands. But since all humans sin by nature, it was necessary for God himself to become one of us and bear the judgment. The apostle Paul explains that God "made him who had no sin to be sin for us, so that in him we might become the righteousness of God" (2 Cor. 5:21).

So when the catechism refers to a mediator, it is referring to Jesus Christ, who was both fully divine and fully human (Q&A 15-18). In Jesus Christ, the Son of God and Son of Man, the justice and mercy of God finally come together. By his incarnation, ministry, sacrificial death on the cross, and resurrection, Jesus atoned for our sins. By God's grace Jesus met the demands of justice and paid the penalty for our sin. Forgiveness abounds. Divine wrath is gone. Thanks be to God!

There is more. Jesus Christ has done far more than fix things so we can go to heaven when we die. As mediator he takes on our brokenness and allows us to find God in every experience, no matter how heartbreaking it may be. He has brought God to us in this mortal and often hurtful life. But he also brings us to God, which is the other half of his mediating work. Through Christ, we are presented to his Father as beloved daughters and sons. So we can again know the joy of being in holy fellowship with our Creator every day of our lives.

MY FAITH

The catechism reminds us that to enjoy all of the grace that has been offered to us, God calls us to respond in faith. To be clear, we don't have faith in order to receive the grace of God. Rather, we respond to grace with faith. This is why the catechism doesn't even bring up the subject of faith until it has fully explained the grace of God that atones for our sins in Jesus

Christ. Grace is God telling us in Jesus Christ that he was literally dying to love us. Faith is our way of saying, "I love you too."

As a pastor, I often find myself standing before a bride and groom at their wedding. I am always amazed by the power of the moment when they exchange vows. Each looks the other in the eyes and makes a covenant to always love unconditionally. It always reminds me of the time Jesus stretched out his hands on the cross. That is when God said, "I will always forgive you, no matter what, because I love you. It doesn't matter how far you turn away from me, my arms will always be open to receiving you again." As powerful as this covenant is, no one can enjoy its grace without believing it, without entrusting themselves to it. When the couple at the altar proclaim their vows to love unconditionally, the excitement of the moment is not just that grace is being promised. It's also that the bride and groom believe each other. So they have faith in the grace, and as long as they do, the marriage can handle anything.

Faith is "a wholehearted trust, which the Holy Spirit creates in me by the gospel," says the catechism (Q&A 21). The significance of this phrase is twofold. First, it reminds us that even our trust in God's grace to forgive our sins comes as a gift from the Holy Spirit. We get so lost in our sin that we lose even the ability to believe that God could possibly be so forgiving. But through the Spirit we discover the grace to believe in grace.

Second, these words from the catechism are significant because they stress once again the importance of an individual response to God's love. Everyone who recites this confession affirms that God has granted grace "not only to others but to me also" (Q&A 21). This is the greatest challenge of faith. We can more easily believe that God loves others, or perhaps even all of us collectively. But faith requires each of us to believe that the "gifts of sheer grace" have also been given to "me." We are each the bride to whom the groom Jesus Christ promises, "I will always love you." And we each must believe that such grace could possibly be true.

OUR FAITH

After such a compelling definition of faith, the catechism turns to the Apostles' Creed (Q&A 23)—that ancient statement of faith all Christians affirm. Our faith needs both substance and accountability. We cannot make our restored relationship with God into whatever we want it to be. When the Holy Spirit creates faith in us, it is always the common faith of the church. This is the faith that, over two thousand years of church tradition, has been hammered out on the anvil of adversity, debate, and our best theological thinking. Our faith makes it clear that God is not my boyfriend, my co-pilot, my boss, or my self-help guru. Our faith teaches me to claim, "I believe in God, the Father almighty, creator of heaven and earth. I believe in Jesus Christ, his only begotten Son, our Lord. . . . I believe in the Holy Spirit. . . . "

That is why no one stands during worship to recite a personal mission statement. Imagine how awful it would be to hear people saying things like, "I believe that God will help me to succeed" or "I believe that my spouse should be nicer to me." There is nothing worthy of worship in such manipulations of the triune God. Our faith is never in me or in what I want to accomplish in my life. Rather, our faith is in a holy God who is at work in me in the same way he worked in all those who have gone before me.

Which returns us to Q&A 1 of the catechism. If my faith were in me or even in the God I refashioned in my own image, it would only create more anxiety because I would constantly fret that God was not going to be or do what I wanted. The "only comfort" that gets us back on our feet and allows us to stand before God and the world is in the historic faith in the God whose very being is a community of divine love and who wants to enfold us in that community. We can either embrace or argue with this faith, but we cannot manipulate it into a self-serving idol.

Unlike the other confessions of the church, we have no idea who wrote the Apostles' Creed. We do know that the congregations of the persecuted church who long ago discovered a faith worth living and dying for hammered it out amid great adversity. This is our great inheritance. I don't shape it. It shapes me.

CHAPTER 3

OUR THOROUGH SALVATION

(Q&A 26–52)

I sit in the preacher's chair during the Christmas Eve service. Looking out at the congregation, I wonder how many times I have viewed this scene. The sanctuary is as dark as the world around us. But everyone in the pews holds a small burning candle, testifying to the light of a Savior who has come. It's not a lot of light—just enough to see people's comforted faces as they sing "Silent Night, Holy Night."

I know these people well. I have celebrated their weddings, baptized their babies, rushed to the hospital when they were in trouble, and buried their spouses. It occurs to me again that they never look better than they do this night, shining in the light of Christmas.

DOES IT WORK FOR US?

While attending a party, an acquaintance asked me what I was working on these days. In talking about this book, I tried to explain the Heidelberg Catechism, its history, and theological insights. It took a lot of work, and I could tell that he still wasn't getting it. So I just quoted the catechism's first question and its response: "My 'only comfort' is 'that I am not my own but belong—body and soul, in life and in death—to my faithful Savior, Jesus Christ.'"

The man looked puzzled, almost offended. Finally he asked, "And this works for you?"

The question was striking for its rigorous pragmatism. He didn't ask me if what I believed was true, but simply if it worked for me. The assumption beneath this question is that we're our own saviors in life. That's a daunting challenge. So we use whatever works to get life to the right place—education, hard work, exercise, sex, even a sixteenth-century catechism. Whatever works for you. The man at the party was trying to be tolerant of my convictions, but clearly he was dismayed that I believed it a comfort to belong to a Savior. Why, he wondered, would anyone give up control of his or her life?

It's healthy for Christians who have been formed by creedal language to encounter conversations with people who find our faith dubious. The catechism certainly doesn't soften the sharp divide between those who believe and those who do not. To the contrary, it makes the divide very clear. We believe that we need a Savior, and we believe that Savior is Jesus Christ: "He saves us from our sins, and . . . salvation should not be sought and cannot be found in anyone else" (Q&A 29).

We believe this not just because it works for us, but because it's true. Sin has separated us from God, others, and our true created nature. We have fallen into a pit so deep that we can never manage our way back to God. Despite the claims of the cherished childhood song, we cannot climb Jacob's ladder—and neither could Jacob. In Jacob's God-given dream, angels came down the ladder, depicting a pathway of salvation utterly unique to the Christian faith. Our hope comes not from our climb up, but from God's climb down to us in Jesus Christ. Hope descends, and that changes everything.

The catechism will not allow us to reduce the nature of our salvation to a lot of prescriptions, morals, and rules for getting our lives fixed. That would be like giving someone who has fallen into the abyss a three-foot ladder. The truth is that we are in too deep to get back to a life that pleases God—or even ourselves. But the saving God comes looking for us in Jesus Christ. And when Jesus finds us, he gives us his life.

ANOINTED WITH CHRIST

It's telling that all the gospel writers begin their accounts of Jesus' public ministry with Jesus' baptism. Why is that event so important to the gospel story? Jesus' baptism is critical because it depicts Jesus' anointing as the Son of God and agent of God's mission to save the world he loves (Q&A 31). (Christ means "the Anointed One.")

To be anointed is to be set apart for a holy mission. So we can say that Jesus Christ is the mission of God to the world for its salvation. When Jesus was born, it was because the Holy Spirit had come upon Mary (Luke 1:34-35). At Jesus' baptism, in which he identified with us, the Spirit descended on him in the form of a dove (Luke 3:21-22). Then the Spirit drove Jesus into the wilderness, where he faced the temptations common to humanity (Luke 4:1-13). When Jesus later presented his credentials for ministry, he claimed, "The Spirit of the Lord is upon me, because he has anointed me to bring good news to the poor. He has sent me to proclaim release to the captives and recovery of sight to the blind, to let the oppressed go free, to proclaim the year of the Lord's favor" (Luke 4:18-19 [NRSV]; see Isa. 61:1-2). Day after the day the Spirit drove the incarnation deeper, identifying salvation in the God who descended to be with us.

Because Jesus our Savior binds us to himself, we "share in his anointing" (Q&A 32). Whenever we witness to Jesus and follow the pattern of his life, whenever we offer ourselves for others as he offered himself for us, and whenever we live by the vision of God's coming kingdom, we live out our "anointing" as agents of God's mission. That's what it means to be a Christian—to be joined in our baptism with the Anointed One.

So when Christians speak about our mission in life, it is not primarily to be a doctor, homemaker, or candlestick maker. Nor does our mission have its origin in our personal strategic plans for life. Primarily, our mission is to Jesus Christ.

Just as the Holy Spirit was the agent of Christ's incarnation, binding him to us, so the apostle Paul makes clear that the Spirit is our means of sanctification. We are sanctified, made holy, by being grafted into the life of our holy Savior. Only the Spirit can do this for us. Only then are we able to participate in Christ's anointed mission. And only then do we realize that our true mission is to bear witness to what Christ is doing wherever we are and whatever we are doing.

It's a mistake to think that Christ completed his work with his sacrificial death on the cross and that, as forgiven people, it's now our turn to take over for him. The risen and ascended Savior continues his anointed mission of bringing the world back to God. He calls us to participate in this work, to throw our lives into it. But we never take over for the Savior. As the catechism reminds us, he is "our only high priest who has delivered us by the one sacrifice of his body, and who continually pleads our cause with the Father" (Q&A 31).

That's good news. If Jesus Christ is our only high priest, then it does not fall to us to decide whether we want to be merciful or whether the church should forgive sins. We are anointed only to announce the forgiveness granted by the high priest.

We add nothing to our salvation by burning ourselves out in ministry and mission. We participate in Christ's anointing by confessing the sufficiency of his one sacrifice, living in the freedom it offers, and sharing its blessing with others. Human efforts at ministry can save no one. Saving the world is ultimately Christ's work, not ours.

Jesus Christ, our high priest, continually pleads our cause with his Father. We participate in this gracious anointing as beloved sons and daughters of God. In part this means that Christ makes our prayers to his Father perfect. Beloved children don't worry about the appropriateness of how they address a parent. When my son wants to borrow my keys to the family car, he doesn't say, "O thou from whose loins I sprang, I humbly beseech thee for the means of transport." Nope. He just asks what is on his heart, trusting that I love him. Whether we pray correctly or incorrectly, Christ always intercedes. Q&A 31 teaches also that we can stop worrying about the day the Father considers us a lost cause. The Savior "continually pleads our cause." He is anointed for this work. We participate in his anointing by continuing to receive this grace.

ADOPTED INTO THE TRIUNE FAMILY

Twentieth-century theologian Karl Barth claimed that "every conception and presentation of a God who is not this three-in-one God [described in the catechism], however beautiful and profound it may be, can only set up an idol, a false image of God."[7] The catechism isn't interested in presenting God in the abstract, but always as the Creator God, as Father, Son, and Holy Spirit—a specific community of divine love. And this triune love is revealed to us in very specific ways.

Creation is a sheer act of love, not a necessity. In the beginning the holy *ruach*, which can be translated as the "breath of God" or "wind from God," shoved aside the darkness and chaos, creating light and beauty in their place. *Ruach* can also be translated as "Spirit." So from the beginning creation has been part of the work of the Spirit. The Gospel of John reminds us that the Word, Jesus Christ, was with God and was God from the beginning (1:1). "All things came into being through him, and without him not one thing came into being" (1:3, NRSV). The birth of the Savior was not an afterthought. From the beginning the triune God has been the creative force in our life, saving us from darkness and chaos. And all of this is born out of holy love.

Love is always and only a choice. It wasn't necessary for God to create the world or even your individual life. But the amazing grace is that God works in specific and not abstract ways to reveal his love. God responds to us the way all good parents respond to their children.

Still working out of the architecture of the Apostles' Creed, the catechism describes the Creator as caring profoundly for the world he made. And we can trust God's purposes and actions because everything comes "by his fatherly hand" (Q&A 27). The Reformed tradition refers to this as the providence of God. It means there is nothing in all of creation—its history, present, or future—that is beyond the reach of God. On the contrary, God "rules" even the "leaf and blade." We find that a great comfort. It would drive us wild with anxiety to consider what it would mean for anything in heaven or on earth to be outside the providential rule of God. For one, it would mean that God is not really God. And it would mean that some creatures have the power to resist the Creator's purposes.

The catechism goes on to state that God also rules over both "rain and drought, fruitful and lean years . . . health and sickness"—which raises difficult questions. We wonder why the ruling God who loves creation would permit droughts, lean years, diseases, and more. These "why" questions go back at least to the laments of Job in the Old Testament. And, like Job, we keep asking them, finding human responses unsatisfactory. Then God meets us in the whirlwind, and we realize it's not why but Who that's important (Job 38-42). We are asking our questions to the almighty, triune God—again, as beloved children.

That doesn't resolve the why questions for us any more than it did for Job. But it is where the doctrine of providence always leads us: back to God. "All things, in fact, come to us not by chance but by his fatherly hand." We may begin with gratitude for the wonderful things that have come to us, or with lament and confusion over the pain of life. But either way we end with "his fatherly hand." I would rather be in that hand confused than left on my own to respond to disaster.

Q&A 26 of the catechism prepares us for the doctrine of providence by teaching that God "will provide whatever I need for body and soul." He is "able to do this because he is almighty God." He "desires to do this because he is a faithful Father." And he "is my God and Father because of Christ the Son." The Holy Spirit has adopted us into the Son's beloved relationship with the Father, giving us a place in the triune Family. We are cherished daughters and sons of the Father.

Drawing from the parable of the prodigal son, the early church theologian Irenaeus explained it this way. He described the Spirit and the Son as the two arms of the Father who rushes down the road to embrace the returning prodigal. In those arms we find ourselves restored to our created family identity. We do not become part of that triune Family because we finally figured out it was time to return to God. At best that would make us a servant in the Father's house. No, we are in the arms of the Father because he reached out to us with the Spirit and the Son.

In order to understand our adoption into the family of the triune God, we must turn again to that key story of Jesus' baptism. As the story goes, John the Baptist had been warning people about the coming Messiah, who would bring judgment and unquenchable fire. So the people who heard John's preaching would repent and be baptized by him. (This was very different from Christian baptism. It was a liturgical act by which people tried to ritualistically wash away their sins. It would be more comparable today to our prayers of confession.) One day Jesus appeared on the shores of the Jordan River, where John was preaching, and told him that he wanted to be baptized. This stunned John, who said he was unworthy to baptize Jesus. They argued a bit. But Jesus won the argument, as he always seems to do, by saying, "It is proper for us to do this to fulfill all righteousness" (Matt. 3:15).

So we are not made righteous by getting our lives cleaned up. We are made right by a Savior who comes alongside us in the futility of trying to make ourselves right. And instead of judging us, he identifies with us. He joins repentant sinners in the waters of baptism. As the catechism says, "during his whole life on earth, but especially at the end, Christ sustained in body and soul the wrath of God against the sin of the whole human race" (Q&A 37). Or, as the apostle Paul puts it, "God made him who had no sin to be sin for us, so that in him we might become the righteousness of God" (2 Cor. 5:21). All of that culminates on the cross, but it begins with Jesus' birth and is dramatically depicted in his baptism.

Then watch what happens. As Jesus steps out of the Jordan, the skies open up. What falls down is not fiery judgment, but the Spirit descending like a dove. And a voice from heaven says, "This is my Son, whom I love [or 'the Beloved']; with him I am well pleased" (Matt. 3:17). It is incredibly significant that Jesus is not called beloved until his baptism. His identification with humanity is so complete that we can hear heaven calling us beloved as well. Heaven is so pleased—not because we finally got our lives cleaned up, but only because the dearly loved Son of God has come to be one of us and bear our sin. In him the triune God takes decisive action to save the world he made.

By this grace of Christ, the catechism teaches, we are now the adopted children of God (Q&A 33). We have becomes heirs of God and joint heirs with Jesus Christ (Rom. 8:17). After receiving this grace, we spend our lives learning what it means to be adopted into the love shared by the Father, Son, and Holy Spirit.

One night my father, who was a pastor, brought home an eleven-year-old boy whose parents had died of a heroin overdose. His name was Roger. His mother had sometimes worshiped with our church. Dad did all that he could to intervene in her and her husband's addiction. But late one night Roger called my father to say that he couldn't wake up his parents. After the coroner took the bodies away, it soon became clear that Roger had no other family. So Dad told the police that he would take Roger in for the night. Somewhere along the way home, my father decided to adopt Roger. I can't imagine the conversation that must have taken place with my mother about this. All I know is that my older brother and I were awakened, introduced to Roger, and told that he would be our brother from now on.

Roger didn't earn his way into our family. He didn't even ask for us. It was solely the grace of my parents that drew in this scared, lost soul. In a moment he became my parents' heir and my joint heir. But while the grace was freely given, it was about to overhaul Roger's life.

Strict personal piety was a strong thread in the fabric of my family's life. We had lots of rules. My older brother and I used to think that our parents never met a rule they didn't like. But as the child of heroin addicts, Roger had never met a rule. That was about to change.

Most of the changes in Roger's life came through the patient teaching of my mother. For years the most common phrase I heard at the dinner table was, "No, no, Roger. We don't do that here." She taught Roger table manners, sharing, civility, kindness, and how to do the dishes. She did so because she wanted him to know how her cherished sons were expected to act.

It took Roger a while, but he made the changes expected of members in our family, and he made them out of gratitude to my parents, whom he knew had saved his life. To be clear, he didn't have to make those changes in order to be in the family. He made them because he was a beloved son.

This is what it means to be adopted into the family of the triune God. It overhauls our identity. With a new understanding of who we are as beloved daughters and sons, we then learn how to act like our joint heir, Jesus Christ. Learning the spiritual disciplines is an act of faith, and faith always follows grace.

Roger was killed in Vietnam. He died heroically for his country. But everyone in our family knew that he also sacrificed his life because he knew our parents were already so pleased with him. No one can give so sacrificially without being loved so thoroughly. The frightened child my parents adopted made his way through all of my mother's table lessons and into the depths of her love. Along the way he was transformed into a hero.

I think of this often when I stand at the Lord's table and offer communion to church members. One after another they come forward to receive the sacrament. Some are tempted to bring their anger, fear, and cynicism. I can almost hear the Holy

Spirit saying, "No, no, we don't do that here." Others are paying attention to the grace of being adopted as God's sons and daughters. They are so overwhelmed by having a place at the table that they find the faith to act like God's beloved children.

Protestants have long asserted that the elements of bread and wine do not change at the table. Right. But we have not with equal vigor claimed that the people who receive communion do change, which is a far more impressive miracle.

A SALVATION THAT SETS US FREE

Three times in this section of the catechism we are told that salvation in Jesus Christ is about experiencing freedom (Q&A 31, 34, and 38). Jesus frees us from sin and from the judgment of God on us because of sin. But Jesus also frees us from the tyranny of the devil, who robbed us of the freedom to be the children of God we were meant to be. Perhaps best of all, we can continue living in this freedom because Jesus, the great High Priest, keeps it for us. He continues to forgive our sin, preventing us from being so addicted to it again that we cannot repent and walk in freedom.

The Greek word for *forgive* that the New Testament uses is synonymous with the word for *freedom*. To be forgiven is to be set free to live as the beloved children of God. We can now follow Jesus Christ. We are no longer imprisoned by guilt and shame. The door of the cell marked "Judgment" has been thrown open. That was God's choice, fulfilled in the atoning life and sacrifice of Jesus Christ. But it's now up to us to walk out of the cell of guilt and shame.

The primal sense of judgment we feel before the holy God leaks into a habit of judgment on ourselves and others. I once made a pastoral visit to one of the new mothers of our congregation. When I arrived at her hospital room the day after the baby was born, I discovered her weeping. I thought maybe these were tears of joy. But she was crying because the doctors had just administered the Apgar test, and they had given the baby only an eight on a scale of one to ten. The mother said, "He's only one day old, and he's already gotten his first B-."

From our first day the judgments just keep coming. We are judged by our friends, teachers, coaches, bosses, and spouses. We are judged by our parents when we are children, and by our children when we become parents. Worst of all is the judgment that keeps showing up in the mirror. And the judgments are seldom that we are good enough.

To be set free from God's judgment by Christ centers our lives and renews our identity of being the beloved of God. So the judgments of the world around us are no longer binding. That doesn't mean we're not accountable to others, or that those who have some authority in our lives cannot help us by telling us when we're headed in the wrong direction. But it does mean that no one can say "not good enough" to a life Jesus was dying to love.

I reminded the mother of the newborn of the last time she took communion at our church, which was just the previous week. As she received the sacrament into her life, the means of grace was already making its way to her child. And that grace will always be available to him. Clearly he's going to need it just as much as the rest of us.

We can define our lives as being at the center or at the boundaries of a circle. If we are centered in Jesus Christ, we are free to maintain rather porous boundaries because we know that the center will hold. We are not defeated by our failures or overwhelmed by our sins. We realize that the holiness of the church is located in Christ and not in its members. So we can handle disagreements in the church without anxiety.

But if we live at the boundaries, we worry constantly about who is right and who is wrong. Instead of centering our confidence in the grace of Christ, we fret that our sins and failures will place us outside that grace. Instead of seeing the church as a haven for sinners saved by grace, we make judgments about who is in and who is out. But Jesus did not go to the cross to keep us from his grace.

HOW LOW SALVATION DESCENDS

The descent of God in Jesus Christ began with Jesus' incarnation, continued in Jesus' baptism, and found its lowest depths in Jesus' crucifixion and death. There is a reason for that.

The catechism reminds each of us that on the cross Christ "shouldered the curse which lay on me, since death by crucifixion was cursed by God" (Q&A 39). Those who are cursed in the Bible are destined to wander through life marked by their failures. In the story of the Fall, God curses the serpent that brought temptation. God curses Adam and Eve, who succumbed to the temptation. And God curses Cain after he killed his brother Abel. The serpent slithers out of paradise on its belly. Adam and Eve lose much of the life they enjoyed in fellowship with the Creator. And Cain becomes a "restless wanderer on the earth" (Gen. 4:12).

Our sin against God, which is at the root of everything hurtful we do, destines us to spend our lives wandering—continually searching for a place to belong once again. Since this sin also alienates us from our primary family relationships, we think we have to keep moving along to find replacements for these needed components in life. We live in a day when it is not only easy to move along, but it's actually encouraged. We're supposed to leave home to get a job or go to college; then we're supposed to leave that to go to either graduate school or wherever the best job is waiting. And after spending a bit of time there, if a better job appears in a new town we're encouraged to leave the old one, along with all the relationships that once appeared so promising but now seem so typically flawed. We might as well all have our names legally changed to Cain.

The issue isn't that we should never move along. Rather, it's what motivates so many of us to constantly move, to never settle down, to never truly commit ourselves to a particular community. Our problem is that we have taken alienation deep into our souls.[8] Even if we do not physically move to another town or job, we're constantly wandering around in search of new experiences or relationships. We may wander into the next self-improvement or weight loss program, a new romance, a new academic degree, or even a new church. But the catechism wants to make it clear that we'll keep searching because we are cursed to wander as a result of our sin. We'll never be satisfied no matter where we look or where we go. That's how the Bible understands a curse.

Often we experience this curse as guilt. We know what we have done and what we have left undone. We feel sin's consequences every day as we wander from one unsatisfying experience to another. We always hope the next thing or person can remove the curse so we can finally settle down in the garden we have been given. But that never happens. The cursed guilt drives us onward. We abandon what we know and have corrupted in our futile search for forgiveness in the next relationship or gadget or job or toy.

But God's curse never eradicates grace. God clothes naked Adam and Eve before sending them from the garden. When Cain laments the curse on his life, the Lord marks him so that it's clear he still belongs to God. So from the beginning God made it clear that he would not abandon us to the curse we have earned. This is why the Son of God has entered our confused and aimless meandering lives.

Jesus once healed a crippled man by telling him that his sins were forgiven (Mark 2:5). As he states in other passages, he forgave the paralytic not because all illness is caused by sin. Rather, Jesus forgave him because nothing is as crippling as guilt. And until we believe that our sins are forgiven, we will never be able to walk as Jesus' disciples; we will never be able to follow him all the way home to God.

In his death on the cross, Jesus shoulders the curse that shadows our lives—his body crippled in the process. Crucifixion was not just a Roman technique for execution. Among Jews, death by hanging on a pole was considered the ultimate curse under God (Deut. 21:23). So the catechism wants us to know that Jesus' death didn't just pay the debt we owed for breaking the law's commands. It also removed the curse of our guilt. We don't have to remain restless, crippled nomads. We can stop pin-balling our way from one experience or relationship to the next. Jesus Christ bears the cursed guilt for us. We are no longer Cain.

While hanging on the cross Jesus laments, "My God, my God, why have you forsaken me?" (Matt. 27:46). These are certainly the most haunting words of the Savior's suffering. They articulate precisely that it's in taking on our God-forsakenness that Jesus becomes our Savior. So we are not abandoned to our cursed guilt. Jesus entered our God-forsakenness so that we might be embraced by the Father. We never again need wander through life alone in a cursed, aimless search. Just as the prodigal before us, we have returned to the arms of our Father.

The catechism also echoes the Apostles' Creed affirmation that after Jesus Christ died "he descended to hell" (Q&A 44). But then it offers a way for us to understand it. While this statement has been in the creed almost from the beginning, we have not always been clear about what it means. It is important to remember that neither the Heidelberg Catechism nor the Apostles' Creed state that the Savior descended "into" hell. Rather, they claim that he descended "to" hell. The catechism interprets this to mean that in Jesus' experience of "attacks of deepest dread and . . . anguish"— throughout his life but especially on the cross—he endured our alienation and judgment from God. In other words, no matter how low or hellacious life may become, we have a Savior who has already descended to that place and is waiting there for us. We cannot sink lower than our Redeemer, Jesus Christ.

But Jesus Christ did not descend to hell just to keep us company. As always, he came to save us. He came down in order to bring us up, to bring us into the communion of Father, Son, and Holy Spirit.

HOW HIGH SALVATION ASCENDS

It may seem strange that the catechism devotes only one question and answer (Q&A 45) to the central fact on which our salvation depends: Christ's resurrection. But rather than as a final step, it sees the resurrection as the first decisive step in a journey that takes Jesus, and us, to glory. Nor is the catechism concerned with exactly what happened in the garden tomb. Instead, as always, it asks what "benefit" the resurrection brings to us.

No one is an unbeliever when it comes to death. We may try to ignore this stark reality, but it always lurks in the back of our minds. If death comes too soon—and when it comes for someone you love, it's always too soon—we may be surprised. But we shouldn't be. Death is simply the mark of being a creature, and life gives us plenty of practice with death-like experiences along the way. Throughout life we constantly experience the death of relationships, jobs, and our physical and mental capacities.

Christianity does nothing to prevent either death or the many losses of life. Instead it offers us the miracle of resurrection.

We see a foreshadowing of this hope in the resurrection of Lazarus. When Lazarus became deathly ill, his sisters summoned Jesus to come quickly to heal him. But, we are told, although Jesus loved Lazarus and his sisters, he did not hurry to rescue him (John 11:5-6). Some Bible translations state that Jesus tarried because he loved them. Out of the abundance of his compassion, our Savior wanted to reveal something more powerful than postponing death. He was ready to reveal his power to raise the dead.

Finally arriving at the tomb where his beloved friend lay buried, Jesus stood outside it and called Lazarus to come forth from it. It's important for us to notice that the Savior did not go into the tomb. That's often what we want once we've settled into our own tombs of despair and loss. We just want Jesus to comfort us. But Jesus doesn't like tombs. He didn't even stay in his own very long. Tombs are places of dread, loss, and death. They're not places to find comfort. So Jesus will not help get us comfortable with our final enemy. Instead, the Resurrection and the Life stands outside the doors of death and calls us to new life. Our Savior has opened the door. He calls us to leave our tombs, just as he will call us from the tomb in the last day.

After his own resurrection from the tomb, Jesus Christ helped his disciples to see that his ministry is about so much more than providing comfort or ease in this mortal life. In rising from the dead he overcame the finality of death and all the death-like experiences we face in life. This astonished the first disciples—and it overwhelms us too, once we grasp its power. As the catechism teaches, "we too are already raised to a new life" (Q&A 45). Yes, though our mortal bodies still die, there will still be a future resurrection of the body, as the Apostles' Creed promises. But all who live in Christ have already begun to enjoy a new life with God from which we can never be separated, certainly not by death (Rom. 8:38-39). This should make us fearless.

When people joined the church during the first three centuries, they were pledging themselves to be part of a persecuted community. They knew that could cost them their lives. But the church was determined to boldly present its great faith to everyone. So the dilemma of early church leaders was how to make members fearless evangelists in the face of death. In response they developed baptismal liturgies that were essentially funeral services. As a new convert descended into the water to be baptized, the church leader spoke about setting aside old habits, old vices, and the old life. Those being baptized even took off their old clothes. Then, as the church leader placed the new member under the water, he said, "Buried with him in baptism." As the new member stood and began to walk out of the water, the church leader said, "Risen to walk with new life in Christ." As the leader declared how the Holy Spirit clothes us with the virtues of Christ, the new member would put on new clothes.

Once church members received a life they could never lose, it made them fearless to proclaim the gospel boldly. In baptism they had already died to the only life persecutors could take from them. Caesar never understood this: it's impossible to scare people who have already died. So the persecuted church grew until it eventually took over the Roman Empire in the fourth century.

This fearless power awaits all who claim their baptismal identity of a risen life in Christ. We follow Jesus Christ into new relationships, adventures in mission, and pursuits of justice not because we expect to succeed, but because we are not afraid to fail. How bad can failure be? Will we lose something we cherish? Will we lose even our lives? We already gave all of that up on the day we were baptized. And in return we gained a risen life with God that we can never lose.

After Jesus opened his disciples' eyes to their inheritance of eternal life, Jesus ascended into heaven, where he serves as our advocate with his Father (Q&A 49). But that doesn't mean his role is to defend or make excuses for our failures. Rather, it means that he presents us to his Father as himself, and he prays for us while we continue to struggle in the world. This is why the catechism stresses that the Son of God does not shed his humanity after he ascends to heaven (Q&A 47, 48). He brings "our own flesh" into the very presence of God (Q&A 49). So our salvation is secure. We remain the Father's beloved and holy sons and daughters for eternity because we are grafted into Christ's beloved, holy body that is both human and divine. Nothing can pull us out of the hands of God.

Jesus did not finish his work with his resurrection. Nor was the Savior done working after his ascension. He continues to unfold his salvation through the Holy Spirit, "who pours out gifts from heaven upon us his members" (Q&A 51). Among those gifts is the ability we each have to serve the mission of Christ's church. Some of us are teachers, preachers, elders, pastors, or other kinds of church leaders. Some of us are farmers, mothers, lawyers, doctors, and businesspeople. The Spirit empowers all of us to join Christ's ongoing work of pointing to the kingdom of God, to join in bringing this world closer to the world God created it to be from the beginning.

This does not mean, of course, that everything will now go well for us. The catechism acknowledges that we will face "distress and persecution" throughout our lives (Q&A 52). But with the comfort, encouragement, and power of the Holy Spirit within us, we are not only unafraid; we refuse to remain discouraged for long. As the catechism claims, regardless of what we may face in life we maintain the posture of an "uplifted head" (Q&A 52). We refuse to be riveted by the challenges of the day, or even by our failures to respond to them righteously. Though our faith may be weak, and life in this world daunting and dangerous, we keep our eyes on Jesus, the King of Glory who is still at work and will bring in his kingdom at last.

CHAPTER 4

THE SPIRIT AND THE SACRAMENTS

(Q&A 53-85)

I t's Sunday morning. As the choir sings during worship, I look out at the congregation. In the third pew, right-hand side, I see a young couple attending church for the first time after their wedding and honeymoon. They can't keep their hands off each other. At the other end of that pew, I see the widow whose husband I buried last month. This is her first time sitting alone in church in more than fifty years. It occurs to me that it hasn't occurred to the newlyweds that someday one of them will also sit alone in church.

Five pews back is a family that's coming apart at the seams. The wife struggles with alcoholism. The husband, though successful in business, feels like a failure because his marriage is in trouble and he can't get his teenage son to talk to him. The teenager sports a spiked haircut, newly orange, and his posture makes it clear that he's only in church because he has to be.

Behind them I see the couple whose baby girl I just baptized. I imagine they're confident that she's not going to grow up to have spiked orange hair.

Across the aisle sits a man in his seventies. He too is alone. After our worship service he will head to the nursing home to feed lunch to his wife, who has Alzheimer's disease. He does that every Sunday. He will tell her all about the worship service, but she won't know who he is.

A few rows in front of him sit a couple who planned to retire this year, but the poor economy has made that impossible. I would have thought they would be upset about that, but all they seem to want to talk about with me is when our church will get more serious about mission to the homeless.

Just ahead of them sits a single mother whose son is a soldier in Afghanistan. I know that if I do not remember to say something about "those who put their lives in harm's way" in the pastoral prayer, she will again say something to me. But we have talked long enough for me to know that beneath that concern is the constant guilt she feels for being divorced.

The choir finishes. As I walk to the pulpit to say, "Hear the Word of the Lord," how do I address all of those pressing concerns? There is only one Word who can make lives right again. And only the Holy Spirit can carry that needed grace to the unrealistic expectations of the young and to the broken hearts of those who've lived awhile.

After the sermon, the congregation forms a long line as they make their way to the Lord's table, where I wait for them. One *after another our eyes meet. In a split second we remember the lost husband, the family in trouble, the dreams that have fallen apart, the guilt that will not go away. I hold up a broken loaf of bread and say only, "The body of Christ." It's all I can say and all that needs to be said—just enough to offer a taste of grace. But the Holy Spirit can do so much with so little.*

THE COMFORT OF THE HOLY SPIRIT

The Heidelberg Catechism turns now to the third section of the Apostles' Creed, which summarizes the person and ministry of the Holy Spirit. It begins by reminding us that "the Spirit, with the Father and the Son, is eternal God" (Q&A 53).

We have already seen that the very first verses of the Bible provide our earliest glimpse of the Holy Spirit at work. The book of Genesis tells us that at creation a wind from God swept over the face of the deep waters, shoving aside the darkness and chaos, creating light and beauty in their place (Gen. 1:1-2). (The phrase "wind from God"—*ruach* in the Hebrew—can also be translated as the "Spirit of God.") At Pentecost the Holy Spirit again appears as a mighty wind, blowing life into the new church and enflaming the disciples of Jesus Christ with the message of salvation in every language (Acts 2:1-4). Thus, the Spirit has always been our eternal God with the Father and the Son. And the Spirit remains a creative force in our lives, never more so than in bringing God to us and us to God through the salvation of Jesus Christ.

There is an intensely personal nature to the ministry of the Holy Spirit. The catechism teaches each of us to believe "that the Spirit is given also to me" (Q&A 53). The Spirit brings the love and redemption of God through Christ into our individual lives. In other words, God does not just "so love the world" (John 3:16), God also loves you. Through the Holy Spirit, the Creator of the world unfolds more good creation in your life: "Through true faith, [the Spirit] makes me share in Christ and all his benefits, comforts me, and will remain with me forever" (Q&A 53).

So as a pastor, when I consider the diverse needs of the people I serve, I have to trust the Holy Spirit to do for them what I cannot. The Holy Spirit makes them share in Christ's life and receive all the joy of being his joint heirs. By adopting us into the Son's beloved status with the Father, the Spirit restores our created identity as children of God. And nothing can take that away. We can't even take it away from ourselves. That's because the Spirit remains with us forever.

In ways that no human can offer, the Spirit comforts my congregation in their grief, diseases, and hurts over broken relationships. Through the Spirit they receive solace from someone who doesn't just know how they feel, but who has the power to heal and restore their hearts. The Spirit knows how life is. He gradually reveals to us how it can be. And through all the experiences of life, joyful or painful, he engrafts us deeper into the life of Jesus Christ.

DRAWN INTO HOLY COMMUNITY

One of the primary places the Spirit works in our lives is through the community of the church. "From the beginning of the world to its end," the catechism teaches, "the Son of God through his Spirit and Word . . . gathers, protects, and preserves for himself a community" (Q&A 54). This community is what the Apostles' Creed calls "the holy catholic church." (The creed uses a small *c* for *catholic* because it refers to the church universal, which is made up of many denominations and theological traditions.)

By claiming that the Spirit and the Word have been forming a community from the beginning, the catechism wants us to know that the missions of the Holy Spirit and the Son of God are not a divine Plan B. It's not as if God first tried to restore us by giving us the law—which didn't work out so well. Rather, we learn that from the very beginning the triune God intended to graft us into the divine community through the community of the church. This has great significance for the line of people in my congregation waiting to get a taste of grace in the sacrament. They're not in a recovery program for sin addicts. Instead, they're fulfilling what they were created to do from the beginning: they're enjoying communion with God. And only the Son and Spirit can draw them into that divine fellowship.

1. Gathered

Q&A 54 promises three specific actions by the Spirit of God on behalf of the church. First, the Holy Spirit "gathers" us from every corner of the earth and from every walk of life. We come with a host of preferences for how to worship our one Savior, which could mean trouble. But we aren't just gathered. We are gathered in Christ. Through the Spirit, who binds us all to Jesus Christ, we always have more unity than we know how to enjoy. Any time we want to remove the dividing walls that separate Christians, we can (Eph. 2:11-22). Our divisions within the church do not protect our theological integrity. Only the Spirit can do that by drawing all believers to our common center in Jesus Christ.

2. Protected

Second, the catechism promises that the Spirit "protects" the holy community created by God. Oddly, the Holy Spirit does this not by building walls around the church. Instead, as the disciples discovered at Pentecost, the Spirit enables the church to give itself away as it follows Jesus' ongoing mission of redemption for the whole world. Whenever the church becomes insular and fearful of the world, it begins to dry up and wither. But when it sacrifices the life it has known to participate in the new work that Christ is doing, it flourishes.

That doesn't mean the church can forget about theological orthodoxy. The church can't change its message to accommodate the "itching ears" of contemporary society (2 Tim. 4:3). It can't simply tell people what they want to hear. Rather, the church proclaims the biblical message of salvation in Jesus Christ in an ever-changing context.

For example, a time came in the last century when the Reformed Church in South Africa knew that it had to speak against apartheid. It had become clear to the church that the country's longstanding policy of racial segregation and discrimination was antithetical to the gospel of Jesus Christ. A century earlier neither South African society nor the church within it were ready for this missional proclamation. But by the end of the twentieth century, speaking against apartheid was a critical response to injustice, and the church in South Africa could not survive without engaging in this prophetic mission. So it has always been.

The church of the first century did not challenge the institution of slavery. But by the early nineteenth century, many churches in the United States knew it was an injustice that offended Jesus Christ and had to be abolished. The Second Great Awakening, a spiritual revival in American society, began around this time. Churches received tremendous renewal as they proclaimed, in part, that Jesus Christ sets all people free. The church today continues to benefit from the effects of this renewal, born from a Spirit-led mission to society.

The Holy Spirit always protects the church's future as the church lives out Christ's mission in its contemporary context. What a great comfort to the church. The Spirit understands society better than it does. The Spirit knows just when and how to advance the mission of Jesus Christ in each cultural setting. And the Spirit guards the church's identity as God's community follows the Savior into the world.

3. Preserved

The third promise the catechism makes about the ministry of the Spirit is that it "preserves" the church for the Son of God. Having spent an enormous amount of my life studying the history of the church, I can assure you that if there were any institution that deserved to go out of business, it's the church. For more than two thousand years we have revealed our tendency to drive the church into the ditch. Too many times we have been on the wrong side of issues of power, justice, truth, and compassion. But still we have been preserved. Clearly this survival is not our doing. Rather, the Holy Spirit constantly works to renew the church in its mission.

FULLY ALIVE AGAIN

The Holy Spirit is at work gathering, protecting, and preserving the holy community we call the church. This community, the catechism continues, is "chosen for eternal life and united in true faith," and every person in it is a "living member" (Q&A 54). We become fully alive again as members of the church. This is striking. The Heidelberg departs here from its use of "me" language. It claims that my only ability to be fully alive is as I participate in the "us" known as the community created by the Word and Spirit. The church is not a voluntary association to which I choose to belong so I can be with people who share my values and experiences. Rather, it is a community created by Jesus Christ and the Holy Spirit for the mission of bringing the world back to life through communion with God.

Just as we don't get to choose the members of the family into which we are born or adopted, neither do we get to choose our family members in the church. The differences we face within a congregation are only lab experiences for understanding how to follow Jesus' mission in a world filled with conflicting ideas about what is the gospel truth. As the Spirit demonstrated at Pentecost, disciples of Jesus Christ come alive not by being with people who are like us, but by receiving into our fellowship those who speak languages we do not know.

I love it when I am in a church committee meeting that includes both longtime members and graduate students new to the congregation. Frequently one of them will say something, and the other will cock his or her head the way a dog does when it is confused. I always smile when I see this. I know the Holy Spirit uses each voice to help the other members of the church become more fully alive through the "us" of Christian community. That "us" is always authoritative for understanding the "me" who is trying to understand what it means to be a Christian among Christians. As Karl Barth said, the Christ for me is first of all *pro nobis* ("for us").[9]

The "me" finds its cherished value in the "we." There are no Lone Ranger Christians. *My* faith is shaped, molded, and held accountable by *our* faith.

That's why we are still learning from such historical sources as the sixteenth-century Heidelberg Catechism. The Spirit unites not just the church today, but the whole church throughout history. If my faith depended simply on what I find in my heart, it would be tentative and shaky. If, however, it depends on what we believe the Holy Spirit has been doing for thousands of years, it stands on solid rock.

THE COMMUNION OF SAINTS

Thus we share not only in the faith of those who are in the church today, but also of those who have gone before us. It is in this context that the catechism and the Apostles' Creed turn to the church's doctrine of the communion of saints.

By "the communion of saints," the catechism and the creed do not just mean especially outstanding people of faith. They're speaking of all people who have believed over the centuries that they are sinners saved by grace. These members of the church, the catechism tells us, "share in Christ and in all his treasures and gifts" (Q&A 55).

Today the church faces many hard choices about worship styles, mission strategies, and more. But the great communion of saints reminds us that we are not on our own as we make these decisions. It comforts us to know that the Holy Spirit is more invested in the future of the church than we are. If we make mistakes, the Spirit will draw us back to Christ—just as the Spirit did after the Crusades and every other misguided undertaking by God's not-always-so-holy community called the church.

RETURNING TO FORGIVENESS

The catechism has a way of returning to our need for forgiveness from sin. In part this is because it follows the summaries of faith we find in the Apostles' Creed, the Ten Commandments, and the Lord's Prayer—all of which teach us that without forgiveness there is no comfort in life or in death. However, the catechism also keeps returning to this topic because none of us ever moves beyond the need to ask for forgiveness. Yet as many times as it returns to this theme, the catechism never repeats itself. There is always more to learn about the forgiving grace of God.

In this section the catechism makes another remarkable claim: "I believe that God, because of Christ's satisfaction, will no longer remember any of my sins or my sinful nature" (Q&A 56). Earlier on we learn that to be forgiven means we are free from the penalty of our sin; the door to the cell of judgment has been thrown open. Now we discover that the record of confessed sin has been expunged—wiped out. It no longer exists. Not even the omnipotent God remembers it.

Because Jesus Christ satisfied God's judgment on the cross, "God grants me the righteousness of Christ to free me forever from judgment" (Q&A 56). To continue to wallow in guilt over the sins we have confessed to God is essentially to claim that Jesus' atonement for those sins was not satisfactory. It is to claim that our guilt is too great for even Jesus to handle—which is saying we don't really have faith in him after all. So we dare not keep confessing the same sin over and over. When we try this, the merciful God responds, "I don't remember what you're talking about."

Jesus told his disciples to put their hands to the plow and not look back (Luke 9:62). Anyone who looks back, he said, is not "fit for service in the kingdom of God." Faith demands that we dwell neither on our glory days nor on our pain, disappointments, and confessed sins. The only time the Bible ever calls the gathered community to look back is to remember the faithfulness of God. And that is so we will be free to move forward, without a crippling limp, believing that God will also be faithful in the challenges that lie ahead.

Occasionally an anxious parishioner will tell me, "I just want what I deserve." As a sinner among sinners I always respond by gently saying, "No, what you deserve is the last thing you want. What you really want is the grace of God." We all desperately need a gracious God who chooses to forget our sin and instead gives us a wide-open future unfettered by the guilt of the past. We can choose to hang on to our guilt. But as the catechism makes clear, that is not what God does.

God sees us as people made right through the work of Jesus Christ, grafted by the Spirit into Jesus' righteous life. The catechism insists that we see ourselves that way too.

Then the catechism propels us forward. It reminds us that "it is impossible for those grafted into Christ through true faith not to produce fruits of gratitude" (Q&A 64). Here is another wonderful grace that frees us from a pathological focus on our sin: the Holy Spirit plants the seeds of holy fruit in our lives.

To be forgiven of our sin is to be set free for a new future. We are no longer chained by guilt over what we have done and left undone. Instead, we start to be known for our love, joy, peace, patience, kindness, goodness, faithfulness, gentleness, and self-control (Gal. 5:22-23). Everyone who has been forgiven and has therefore received the Holy Spirit has the capacity to bear all these spiritual traits, just as Jesus did.

This fruit comes naturally from the work of the Spirit in our lives. When we do not demonstrate the fruit of the Holy Spirit, it is only because we are pretending to be someone we are no longer. Suppose a member of the church apologizes to me half-heartedly for losing his cool, saying, "I'm sorry for my temper, but that is just who I am." I can smile gently and say, "No, it's not. That is just who you have grown used to being."

THE COMFORT OF THE SACRAMENTS

We need to remember our identity as the beloved daughters and sons of God. The catechism now moves into a wonderful description of how the sacraments nurture that identity:

> The Holy Spirit produces [faith] in our hearts
> by the preaching of the holy gospel,
> and confirms it
> by the use of the holy sacraments." (Q&A 65)

It may come as a surprise to some that the Reformed tradition has always held that the preaching of the Word and the offering of the sacraments belong together. To pull one apart from the other would be to threaten the meaning of both.

The word *sacrament* comes to us from Latin. It means "mystery." Through the church's two sacraments of baptism and the Holy Supper (communion), we receive the same gospel of grace proclaimed through the preaching of the Word. But we receive it mysteriously communicated through an experience.

Like most happily married couples my wife and I begin and end each day with an "I love you," and then we kiss. Why do we bother with the kiss if we have already said, "I love you"? The kiss doesn't communicate anything that was not already in the words. But we're not about to stop kissing. Something would be seriously wrong in our relationship if one of us said, "I already told you that I love you. Do we really need to keep kissing?" And something would also be wrong if either person said, "I don't mind the kissing, but do I really have to keep telling you that I love you?"

When I stand behind the pulpit on Sunday morning, I use words to tell the congregation that Jesus Christ was dying to love them. When I stand in front of the Lord's table, offering them his broken body and poured out blood, I present the sacred kiss that communicates the same thing as the sermon, but in ways that go far beyond the limits of words. And when I offer the sacrament of baptism, I'm doing the same thing: bestowing the grace of God in a way that can be experienced and not just heard.

When we baptize someone, we both proclaim and demonstrate that God has chosen to bring this person into the covenant community that lives by grace. We are saying that the sins of this individual have been washed away not by his or her own efforts, but by the blood of Jesus Christ. And we are saying that he or she will spend the rest of life responding to that extraordinary grace.

After a couple has been dating for a while, one of them eventually takes the plunge and says, "I love you." Maybe this is planned over a candle-lit dinner at a restaurant, or perhaps it's just blurted out. But after the words are spoken, it occurs to the person who said them that a huge risk has just been taken. The relationship has just been placed at a crossroad. Either it will move ahead into intimacy, or you might as well just pay the check and go home because there is no way to stay "just friends" with someone you are in love with. In baptism, God takes the risk—the whole church hears the sacred "I love you." Now we hold our breath and wait for the baptized to say, "I love you too."

When we baptize infants, the congregation holds its breath for a very long time. In most Reformed churches the response comes during adolescence, after an extensive period of training in the faith. Whether we call this step confirmation or public profession of faith, what we are confirming or professing are baptismal vows. This is when young people who were baptized as infants stand in front of the congregation and with their own lips say to God, "I love you too."

As the catechism teaches, we include infants in the sacrament of baptism because it marks them with the grace of God in a way similar to how circumcision marked the children of the Hebrews (see Q&A 74). But we also baptize babies because the act beautifully demonstrates how God bestows his grace and love on us before we even know that we need it or are receiving it. Whether we are baptized as infants or adults, we spend the rest of our lives growing in our understanding of that grace and learning what it really means to tell God, "I love you too."

Having begun our lives as disciples of Jesus Christ through the sacrament of baptism, we are further nurtured in this identity through the sacrament of the Lord's Supper. Every time we come to the table we are met by the Holy Spirit. The Spirit lifts us up to encounter the risen and ascended Savior, Jesus Christ, who is at the right hand of his Father. Then we are overwhelmed to discover that we are having communion with Father, Son, and Holy Spirit. As adopted children we have graciously been given a place at the holy table.

Reformed churches have resisted worrying about how exactly Christ is present at the table. Instead our focus is on being lifted up to our union in Christ (Q&A 76). It is for this reason that we speak about a table rather than an altar. We are not trying to sacrifice Christ again, which would require an altar (Q&A 80). We are gathering as Christ's joint heirs at the family table of God. We are enjoying communion with our triune Family. And as is typically the case at family tables, it is there that we learn what it means to bear our family name.

When I was a boy, my brother and I spent a lot of time with my grandmothers during the summers. One lived in the city and maintained a small but elegant Victorian home. The other still lived on the family farm.

Neither grandmother had very much money, but each got by on Social Security and what her husband had set aside. Both had struggled as young mothers during the Great Depression, which left them with the nagging fear that they could still lose everything. But they responded to this anxiety in dramatically different ways. These differences became acutely clear at their dinner tables.

My city grandmother always served dinner at her dining room table, which she covered in a yellowed lace cloth. Her chipped china was carefully placed around small but polished silver candlesticks. There were always more forks than I could figure out how to use. She taught me that the linen napkin immediately goes in my lap, that I should always stand if a lady approaches the table, and that it is impolite to reach. She made sure to have classical music playing on the stereo built into a massive wood cabinet.

Eating at her table was a bit of a chore. I don't remember any conversations from those dinners. I just remember being dressed up, speaking in soft tones, if at all, and the terrifying fear of spilling my juice on that lace tablecloth.

By contrast, my country grandmother served her meals in the kitchen, since she didn't have a dining room. Her table was always covered with a red-and-white-checked vinyl cloth, which took a spill pretty well. You used only one fork, and if it fell on the floor you just picked it up and wiped it off with a paper napkin. But you had to be fast because a dog named Brownie hovered nearby. We drank from a strange assortment of plastic glasses that bore names such as John Deere or Red Moon Pizzeria. And you never knew who would be at that table. If a neighbor or even a salesperson stopped by near dinnertime, Grandma would insist that he or she stay for dinner.

The conversations at her table were often boisterous—typically there were several going on at the same time. But anytime Grandma would start to tell a story, everyone would listen. When she got to the funny part, she would begin to laugh so hard that she'd slap the table three times as she coughed and the tears rolled down her cheeks.

Again, both women were responding to anxiety—to life in a volatile world. One chose to rise above it by insisting on elegance and refusing to allow her fears to reduce her character. The other chose laughter and joy in each day she had. Significantly, each realized she could choose how to respond to her fears.

Today as I stand behind the table of the Lord, I think often about these two influential women in my life.

My city grandmother would be impressed by how carefully we prepare the communion table with a beautiful cloth and our finest silver. The music is classical. Everyone dresses up and speaks in hushed tones. We stand and sit at the correct times.

And the last thing any pastor wants to do is spill the juice on the tablecloth.

I see much more of our theology for this sacrament, however, in what I learned at my country grandma's table. The Eucharistic feast is all about joy. If you make a mistake or commit a sin, well, that's why we have this sacrament of grace. Strangers are always welcome. And Jesus is so excited to have us all there, in communion with him, that I can almost see him slapping the table three times out of sheer delight. Surely the tears of joy roll down.

Still, I am not about to suggest to our worship committee that we start using a red-and-white vinyl cloth or that we replace the polished silver with plastic vessels. I suppose that is because my city grandmother was also trying to teach me something I don't want to forget. She wanted me to learn how to be elegant. And in my middle age I now think that's also a means of grace. We could certainly use more elegance and civility in our current debates. Receiving grace should make us gracious. And graciousness is exactly what's missing in our struggles within churches, families, and nations. There's holiness in being careful, just as there is in laughter and living with abandoned trust.

We still live in a time of great anxiety. When I serve communion I can almost see my two grandmothers leaning over the balcony of heaven, encouraging us with their counsel for modest elegance or sheer delight. The Holy Spirit calls for both and uses the sacrament to bring these gifts to fruition in our lives.[10]

The fruit cannot grow, however, without the Spirit first casting out all our anxiety with the perfect love of God (1 John 4:18). And that is what we remember—and taste—every time we come to the holy table (Q&A 75). We never come to this table because we deserve to be there. It is always and only a grace. We come to the table because we desperately need the gracious love that is spread upon it.

WHO HOLDS THE KEYS?

I have always been fascinated by how much toddlers like to play with keys. It suggests to me that we're wired to get our hands on those things. They make us feel like people of authority, like people in control. With them we can open and lock doors. The custodian for our church has an impressively large ring filled with keys that dangles at his side. I think of it whenever a discussion comes up about the church keeping the keys to the kingdom of God. The catechism teaches us that there are only two such keys: "the preaching of the holy gospel and Christian discipline toward repentance." With these keys the kingdom of heaven is opened to believers and closed to unbelievers (Q&A 83).

The church has never had the power to make people repent of the sin that separates them from God. It is only the Holy Spirit who convicts us, who makes us lonesome for God. It is only the Spirit who leads us back to the family table. The leaders of a congregation don't gather the church, and they certainly don't keep it pure by excluding sinners. It is the Holy

Spirit's job to determine who should be in the church. The leaders of the church are called only to proclaim the gospel (with guidance by the Spirit) and to receive everyone the Spirit draws back into communion with God.

The early church used to celebrate the Holy Supper every Sunday. But they would excuse those who were not yet baptized and those who were not yet ready to repent of their sins. It would be so grievous to be kept from the table, the church assumed, that the unrepentant would change their ways and do whatever was necessary to get back into communion with God. So excommunication was never meant to be a means of kicking someone out of the church. It was intended to nudge people to repent, or turn back, to fellowship with God. Nonetheless, it is a difficult task. It must be taken on with an enormous amount of humility and capacity for holy surprises. If the church wants to be the light of the world, it needs to get used to attracting a few bugs. However, God creates even bugs, and we need to be ready to welcome anyone who desires to receive the transforming grace of God found in the Holy Supper.

To lead a congregation is to call everyone, including the clergy, to constant repentance of the many things that pull us away from God. And then we need to be ready to fully receive all who have been brought back home by the Spirit. As a pastor, I take great comfort in knowing that the keys to the kingdom are not in my hands but on the belt loop of the Holy Spirit, the true custodian of the church. I am often stunned by those the Spirit brings home to dinner. But then I remember my own sins.

CHAPTER 5

THE GRATEFUL LIFE

(Q&A 86-115)

A young real estate agent sits before her computer at night, knocking herself out to prepare for showing her new clients several more houses in the morning. There's a lot on the line.

She remembers again how much her little single-parent family needs the money that will come if the clients buy one of the houses she shows them. Her twins need new coats and shoes, her car is on its last legs, and she's way behind on her Visa® bill. Since the divorce her parents have kept offering to help, but she's determined to make it on her own.

Despite her resolve, in her bravest moments she confesses to herself that she's lost in a life that's far from what she had dreamed. There aren't too many of those moments, though. She can't afford them. So she just keeps resolving to work harder: "I have to close a deal on a house. If I can sell even one house this month, we'll have enough to get by." She's lost track of how many times she has said that.

One of her twin daughters quietly approaches in pajamas, with a worn teddy bear in tow. Pulling on her mother's sleeve, she pleads, "Can you color with me?" Without thinking, the woman quickly responds, "Not now. Mommy is busy." The little girl understands. But as the mother watches her daughter waddle away with the bear, she curses herself and wipes away a tear. Then she turns back to the computer.

TRYING TO DO GOOD

Most people want to do well at life. Few of us resolve to hurt others, and certainly not those we love the most. But we often fail to do good. The journey through life takes a lot of twists and turns, and it's easy to get lost trying to get back to the right place. That's when we become anxious—and when we run the fastest, even if it's in the wrong direction. Typically, we're running so frantically that we don't even realize we've run over someone we love.

The Heidelberg Catechism has already taught us that sin is anything that separates us from being in communion with God. This includes the resolve to fix life on our own. Most of us cope with sin not by confessing it and casting ourselves on the grace of God, but by trying to manage it the best we can. But the only way we can manage sin is by committing more sin. So, like this young real estate agent, we find ourselves hurting even our own families by trying to provide for them. That's when the judgment starts to flow. And the worst judgments always come from ourselves.

When I teach students at the seminary, I caution them against preaching "bad dog" sermons. When the preacher climbs into the pulpit to denounce the congregation for their many sins, he or she is essentially wagging a finger at them and saying, "Shame on you. Look at what you did." And the preacher's expectation is that, like golden retrievers, the people in the pews will cower and think, "You're right. I did it again."

The problem with such sermons is that the type of people who come to church don't need to be convinced they're bad dogs. They already believe that. But they don't know what to do about it. Parents still have to worry about paying the rent, and they can't color with their children any time they want. But trying to be a good provider has meant they hurt someone they love. So even when we try to do what is good, we still end up as bad dogs.

The grace of Jesus Christ breaks into this common human predicament. Grace doesn't pay the rent for us or show us how to care for our children while keeping up with a demanding job. But it does help us recover the image of God in our lives. That frees us to be ourselves again—beloved sons and daughters of our heavenly Father. Nothing can change that. We still have to make difficult decisions, but we're no longer under the illusion that any of those choices can save us. Now we make decisions as people who know we are already saved by the grace of God. So even when the good we do is flawed, we trust that God will forgive our shortcomings and use our clearly imperfect efforts at being faithful.

I was once blessed with a day in the museums of Florence, Italy. I began by looking at the medieval paintings that were preoccupied with judgment for our sins. The scenes were dark and condemning, the people diminished and dour. I noticed that no tourist spent much time in front of them. Again, we already know we are bad dogs. We don't need even artful reminders of this.

Then I made it to the Renaissance art that had recovered a sense of the beauty of humanity. There I saw Michelangelo's amazing, larger-than-life statue of David. No one wanted to leave. The museum guards had to keep asking the crowd to move along. But we were all stuck. We were staring at an artistic rendering of what it means to be made in the image of God. It wasn't just the physical beauty of a human form that we found so attractive, but Michelangelo's depiction of the human soul adored by God. Michelangelo understood that God loves what he has created. David will forever be known as "a man after [God's] own heart" (1 Sam. 13:14; Acts 13:22). We were looking at the best image of our true selves, and we couldn't take our eyes off it.

That is who Jesus is. But he is not just an artistic depiction of who we should be. Jesus is who we really are, as God sees us, when we respond in faith to God's forgiving grace. Then the Holy Spirit grafts us into the Son's relationship with the Father, making us also the beloved of God.

As is well known, Michelangelo's philosophy of sculpture was that the image was already inside the stone. The artist merely freed it by removing everything that did not belong. That is exactly what Jesus does for us. So when we have been hurt or when we fail at trying to do well, he tells us to just shake it off, like dust from our sandals, and keep moving (Mark 6:11). Neither victimization nor guilt is part of our sculpture. Jesus frees his disciples from carrying around the failures, judgments, and hurts of yesterday.

GRATITUDE

We learn from the catechism that we don't try to do well at life in order to chip away our sins and recover the inner image of God. Jesus Christ has already accomplished that for us and is "restoring us by his Spirit into his image" (Q&A 86). As John Calvin explained in the *Institutes,* every part of our salvation is already complete in Christ by virtue of his obedience for us and the Spirit's invitation to live our life in Christ.

We try to do well not in order to escape slavery to sin, but because we are already free from it. We try to do well because we now have the capacity to demonstrate what people made in the image of God do with their lives. And we are motivated to do this good out of deep gratitude for our freedom. This is why the catechism calls its section on doing good works "Gratitude."

It is impossible to be grateful and angry, cynical, envious, mean, or self-absorbed. Gratitude pushes away those negative emotions. But we can be grateful and loving, devoted, giving, forgiving, and committed to justice. For this reason gratitude may be the best measure of our spirituality. It demonstrates that we've been paying attention to the grace we have received in Jesus Christ, who has restored God's image in us. We were never created to be mean or hurtful. In Christ our great Sculptor has removed all the false images from our lives.

But even our gratitude for this freeing salvation is nurtured by the Holy Spirit. The gratitude we muster in our hearts on our own cannot possibly be strong enough to make us good. Those of us who hang around churches are accustomed to hearing about Jesus going to the cross for our sins. After depicting the horrors of Jesus' crucifixion, a preacher will sometimes say, "See how much your salvation cost our Savior? He did his part. So now it's your turn to demonstrate your gratitude by living a godly life." This assumes that all we need is forgiveness for past sins and that now our own gratitude should be a force powerful enough to drive us to holiness. Essentially, it reduces salvation to a second chance, and it admonishes us not to mess up again. It also leaves Jesus on the cross and places all the current responsibility for holiness on our own shoulders.

There's an obvious problem with this view: We need a whole lot more than a second chance at life with God. We will make just as big a mess of it as we did the first chance. What we need is a risen and ascended Savior who continues to redeem our lives, unfold our salvation, and transform us into men and women who are free to pursue holiness.

So we are always grateful not just for what Jesus did accomplish, but for what he does accomplish through the Holy Spirit in our lives every day. We were saved by grace, but we grow into the Christian life by the grace of a Savior who is not done. Jesus continues to free us to do good. And the Spirit continues to makes our hearts so grateful that we want to do it. None of that happens all at once. Notice how the catechism describes our conversion as an ongoing process of "dying-away of the old self, and the rising-to-life of the new" (Q&A 88).

The catechism describes our gratitude as "a love and delight to live according to the will of God" (Q&A 90). The more grateful we are, the more we delight in the will of God. And the more we follow God's will, the more gratitude we receive for the delight it gives. At the same time, we become "genuinely sorry for our sin" and "run from it" because it pulls us away from the gratitude in which we delight (Q&A 89). This is how we grow toward a life that is pleasing to God. We die to the old self that left us alone and filled us with complaint, and we rise to a new life that is such a holy and delight-filled gift that all we can do is spend the rest of life expressing deep gratitude. This is what the catechism calls "genuine repentance or conversion" (Q&A 88).

Finally, it is important to remember that this life-altering gratitude is so much more than an attitude or theological commitment. It must be grounded in specific acts of praise. In the words of author Ann Voskamp, "I discover that slapping a sloppy brush of thanksgiving over everything in my life leaves me deeply thankful for very few things. A lifetime of sermons on 'thanks in all things' and the shelves sagging with books on these things and I testify: life-changing gratitude does not fasten to a life unless nailed through with one very specific nail at a time."[11] As we discussed earlier, in chapter three, the love of God is not abstract, but specific. We experience true gratitude the same way.

We can trust both God's Word and Spirit for our freedom, new life, and delight-filled gratitude. But God gives us even more. God reveals specific directions to guide our journey through life. We might consider these signposts that help to keep us on track. The Bible calls them the Ten Commandments, and the catechism discusses them in detail.

LIBERATING COMMANDMENTS

John Calvin taught us that the law is written and engraved on our hearts by the finger of God, just as God once wrote it on the stone tablets given to Moses. And Calvin claimed that the law is given not to make us afraid of God, but to provide a means of loving him who is our deliverer and the source of our freedom (*Institutes*, II.vii.12).

So Reformed Christians have never thought of loving God as just an emotional experience. We also love God by devoting ourselves to conforming to God's law, since God's law reveals the good that Christ frees us to do (Q&A 91). This is sometimes referred to as Calvin's third use of the law. The first is to convict us of our sin, and the second is to restrain the actions of evil people who will fear its punishments. But the third use of the law has a positive purpose for "those believers in whose hearts the Holy Spirit already flourishes and reigns. . . . For it is the best instrument for enabling them daily to learn with greater truth and certainty what the will of the Lord is that they aspire to follow" (*Institutes,* II.vii.12). So the Ten Commandments provide a means of keeping our freedom by revealing the will of our Liberator God.

It is incredibly significant that these commandments were given just three months after the Hebrews' great exodus from slavery in Egypt. God heard the cries of his people who were suffering under Pharaoh, and God parted the Red Sea to deliver them. A highway called "The Way of the Philistines" ran along the Mediterranean coast from Egypt to the promised land. It was heavily traveled, with lots of food and water available along the way. It was the fastest route to the promised land. But God knew that as soon as their new life became difficult, his people would sacrifice their freedom and run back to Egypt (Ex. 13:17). So God led his people through "the roundabout way of the wilderness," through the harsh desert where resources were scarce and adversity great. There the Hebrews learned how to have faith in God. And there they received the Ten Commandments that would guide them in the path of freedom.

Every leader in the biblical drama had to find communion with God in the desert, including Abraham, Moses, David, John the Baptist, Paul, and even Jesus. And to this day God still leads us through the wilderness of adversity as we make our way to the promised land—as we become who we were created to be. It is on the hard road that God converts us from slaves to beloved creations of God who know how to walk faithfully on any road.

The commandments teach us how to keep our freedom. For that reason they begin with an important prologue: "I am the LORD your God, who brought you out of the land of Egypt, out of the house of slavery" (Ex. 20:2). Here God clues us in to the purpose of the law. God tells us, "Remember who I am and what I have done. I have set you free." This provides the interpretative key to everything that follows: we have a God who liberates us and who will not tolerate our slinking back to slavery.

As a pastor I remain confounded by how many people prefer the misery they know to the mystery they don't. Logically, mystery is better than misery. But the human soul has a way of reflecting the Hebrews' tendency to look over their shoulders at Egypt while on the hard and mysterious road to freedom. The law, however, calls us forward.

NO OTHER GODS

If you find yourself stuck in a job you hate but need in order to afford a lifestyle you also don't like, that is not God's doing. Don't blame God if you have settled into a dreary mediocrity in your relationships. And don't ever think that it's God's idea for you to suffer under taskmasters who enslave you to a life without mission, passion, and hope. God never calls you to that. But that is always where life ends up when we serve any other god. This is why the first commandment claims, "You shall have no other gods before me" (Ex. 20:3). Whenever we break this commandment, we always find ourselves back in miserable slavery (Q&A 94). God's law is a means of grace. God found us when we were enslaved by our sin; he heard our cries and delivered us. That is what the exodus was about, what the Ten Commandments are about, and what the ministry of Jesus Christ is all about. They are all part of the same fabric of redemption.

We see this pictured in our baptism as well. Baptism is a way of remembering that we, too, have passed through the water and have begun a mysterious journey with God in freedom. Some of us pass through the water as adults, just like the Hebrews who walked through the Red Sea. Others are carried across in the arms of parents, like the Hebrew babies. But all of us who call ourselves Christians are on the journey somewhere between slavery and the promised land.

NO IDOLS

Since God does not always make his presence apparent when we are in the desert of life, we sometimes become frightened and tempted to turn to an idol for comfort. We like idols because, like the golden calf (Ex. 32), we can shape them with our own hands. And we think that they will make no demands of us. But they do. Every idol commands that we sacrifice our freedom and head back to Egypt. This is why the second commandment forbids idolatry (Ex. 20:4-6).

On the road to freedom we learn to leave behind the idols that deceive us by promising shortcuts to the promised land. We do not need to buy something else, get another promotion, fall in love with someone, or accumulate more money. Those things are not bad in themselves, but they become deadly to our souls when we start to believe they can save us. That's when they become idols. And the best that any idol can do is to help us cope with slavery. But the mysterious liberator leads us with a vision of how good life can be.

In keeping with Scripture, the catechism is also concerned that we not attempt to make an image even of the true God (Q&A 97). That is because we inevitably turn those images into idols. This is an important reminder for churches to keep in mind as we distinguish between idols and religious symbols such as the cross, the communion table, stained-glass windows, other sanctuary furnishings, and church buildings themselves.

Symbols are designed to help us worship God. They point to God, while idols are ends in themselves. We can always tell if a symbol has become an idol by asking ourselves if we can get by without it. It is not our cherished sanctuaries that keep us free, but the preaching of the Word within them (Q&A 98). Be careful, the catechism, warns. Only the Word of God can deliver us.

LIVING WITH THE SACRED

The third commandment states, "You shall not take the Lord's name in vain," and the fourth tells us to "Remember the Sabbath and keep it holy" (see Ex. 20:7-8). Both mean that without worship all of life becomes profane. With worship all of life becomes sacred.

What does it mean to take the Lord's name in vain? Does it mean that God is so bothered by cursing that he made it third on the list of ten deadly sins? There's probably more to it than that. Does it mean there's something so celestial about God that it's best not to call on him or even to invoke his name lest you contaminate it with your mundane issues? The Hebrew people were quite concerned about that. They were so worried about profaning the name of God that they wouldn't even say God's revealed name of *Yahweh.* Instead they would say *Adonai,* which essentially translates as "you know who I'm talking about, but we can't say his name."

Do we really profane a holy God by speaking his name in the context of our little problems? Of course not. Actually, what is more typical of us is not that we misuse the name of God, but that we no longer use it at all. We don't seriously invoke God's name when it comes to our needs or the needs of the world. Oh, we may pray about these things sometimes—and we probably even believe God could do something about them. What we doubt is that he will. We think that God just doesn't want to get involved. And that is to take the Lord's name in vain.

According to the first commandment, God's name is also "the LORD . . . who brought you out . . . of slavery." This is the God who delivers, the God of your salvation. In the Hebrew mentality, the name of an individual proclaimed the character of that person. So to take God's name in vain is to ignore his character as the Savior who is very involved. It is for this same reason that Christians pray "in the name of Jesus." Every time we call on that name, we are proclaiming that the work of Christ is to save and deliver us.

Any time you think you can find a little salvation through your own work, you are in grave danger. The danger is this: if you fail, or worse yet if you succeed for a while, then you're stuck with yourself for a god. That destines you to the profane existence of journeying through life as if the solution to every problem is to get busy.

When you are your own god, life knows no mystery or awe. Nothing amazes, astonishes, or overwhelms you. And that is a small and very sad way to live. It flattens your soul. It leads you back to slavery in Egypt.

Ironically, to be frantic with busyness is a lazy thing. It avoids the hard work of calling on the Lord's name and looking for his involvement. As the catechism claims, to invoke God's name is to glorify him in all our words and works (Q&A 99). It is not saying that Christians shouldn't work hard. It's saying that if we're not praying about our work, we're not working hard enough.

God is involved. That's his character. It's in his name. To pray to see God's saving involvement is to seek a divine importance to our schedules and routines. We have classes to attend, sales to make, reports to write, floors to clean, children to tend, planes to catch, and one more customer to satisfy. If all that is just stuff we've got to do, our lives are rather profane. But if we are looking for God's presence in the midst of it, then all of life becomes an opportunity to encounter the sacred.

SABBATH KEEPING

So how do we see God's presence in our lives? The fourth commandment speaks to this: "Remember the Sabbath and keep it holy."

Does that mean we should go to worship on Sunday? Actually, yes, I think it does (see Q&A 103). But not for the reason we might assume. Remember, the commandments are signposts to freedom. Their fundamental theme is not slavish obedience, but deliverance and salvation. If we worship because it's our duty, we're missing the point. We don't worship because we have to, but because we get to. Worship is our chance to see what's going on from heaven's perspective.

We are called to keep the Sabbath rest because God himself rested from his work on this day—not because he was tired, but to enjoy his work and say, "It is good." This means that creation culminates not in work, not even in God's work, but in doxology. So worship is our opportunity to see the glorious creativity of all of those ordinary days in-between.

We sometimes say, "On Sunday we go to church." But that isn't quite right. Christians are the church all week long, in whatever places we have been sent to work. In the words of the catechism, "every day of my life I rest from my evil ways, let the Lord work in me through his Spirit, and so begin in this life the eternal Sabbath" (Q&A 103).

We gather to worship in order to see that God is with us in our work, bringing the eternal blessings of heaven to our little part of earth. The Sabbath is not our day off from frantically toiling for an employer so we can frantically take care of stuff at home. And it is not given so we can catch our breath in order to "get back at it" on Monday. That assumes that life culminates in work.

The literal translation of *Sabbath* is "give it a rest," "stop," or even "cut it out!" Worship is God's great interruption of our busyness. Too often we're concerned about how hard our work is or whether it's fulfilling, about the supervisor who doesn't appreciate us, the salary that's not nearly enough, or the children we can't make perfect. On the Sabbath we hear God say, "Cut it out! Lift up your eyes and see what incredible blessings you have received."

From the beginning we have been created to live in a specific rhythm: six days of work followed by a day of rest. All creation from humanity to animals and even the dirt of our fields has been created with the need to rest. We need this rest not just to recover strength, but to recover the goodness of life. When we resist this created rhythm of life, it is not long before we find ourselves enslaved by work. We know this has happened when instead of joining God in saying, "It is good," all we ever seem to say is that it's just not good enough.

The early church changed their day of worship from the seventh day of the week to the first. Every Sunday they wanted to rehearse the joyful surprise of the resurrection. Week after week, year after year we join the followers of Christ around the world in affirming that the Savior who defeated death can also bring new life to us. In the words of the apostle Paul, "He who began a good work in you will carry it on to completion" (Phil. 1:6). This is why our Sabbath observances always have a note of celebration to them. God is good, and in worship we sing and pray and proclaim our thanksgiving. Only then do we recover the goodness of our own lives.

In 1964 the French philosopher Jean Vanier established a community for people with intellectual disabilities. He called this community "L'Arche," which means "the Ark." Vanier quickly discovered that people with intellectual disabilities, robbed of all pretense, demonstrate the most essential traits of the human condition common to all of us. For example, he said, humans need to give praise in order to stay healthy. One of the most important things people in the L'Arche community do is celebrate. They celebrate holidays, birthdays, accomplishments, anniversaries, and anything else they can think of. If a week goes by without a celebratory event, they make one up. Why? Because suffering does not have the final word.

In worship we choose to enjoy and celebrate the goodness of God in the life we have.

REVERING LIFE

Now the catechism leads us to the fifth commandment: "Honor your father and your mother" (see Q&A 104). And to the sixth: "You shall not murder" (see Q&A 105). Both commandments call us to revere life—our own life that has been shaped and molded by our parents, and the lives of people around us.

Today we have become familiar with the language of dysfunctional families, and many people are engaging in courageous therapeutic journeys that bid them to return to their anger at Mom or Dad. Yet the fifth commandment defiantly directs us to honor our parents. The easiest interpretation of this law is to say that it applies only to the many parents who did an honorable job. These good parents certainly made mistakes, but they also made considerable sacrifices and knocked themselves out to demonstrate their love for their children. But never trust the easiest interpretation of Scripture. This commandment is not conditional. We are not told to honor those who do well at parenting. We are told simply to honor Father and Mother, which includes all fathers and mothers, that our days may be long in the new places to which God is leading.

This is the first commandment that comes with a promise: long days in a new place. Remember, the commandments were given to people who were on a journey— between Egypt and the promised land, between a former place and a new place. And the fifth commandment serves as a signpost to help us make it to that new home. But, it cautions, unless you honor the home from which you have come, you'll never be able to receive the home to which you are heading.

Let's be clear about what this commandment says. We are not told to stay at home with Mother and Father, to agree with them, or to assume their values. Frankly, we are not even told to love Mother and Father. We are told to honor them.

To honor means to give people due importance and respect, to acknowledge their significance. To honor your parents means that you realize your life was shaped, for better and for worse, by those who raised you.

Parents give us our names and identities. They nurture us and provide for our needs. They teach us right from wrong. They set the boundaries for the gardens in which we grow. These are world-creating, life-shaping functions. Some parents excel at them. Others are just awful. But, in either case, unless we honor their influence in our lives, we will never be free to face our future. The catechism cautions us to be patient with our parents' failings; otherwise we will spend the rest of our lives in an enslaving reaction.

To honor the past doesn't mean we condone it. It means we see it for what it is and realize that God has used it to shape us. Both pain and joy are creative. Both must be honored as experiences that give us our life's story. For those of us still focused on the flaws of Mother and Father, it could be that those flaws are our best preparation for receiving the flawed relationships of the future. For those who believe Mother and Father did a pretty good job, it could be that the most honorable way to say thanks is to live as someone who knows how to give love to others.

Every week the worship bulletin of our church contains a brief announcement of who donated flowers for the sanctuary that Sunday. Many times the flowers are in honor of someone's father or mother. That's all the notice says. But between the lines often lies a drama. There's a man in our church whose father left when he was a teenager. For many years the son resented his dad. This anger bound him and put a lien on other relationships. He was afraid to trust. Even when the son became an adult, his self-esteem remained stuck as that of the abandoned teenage boy. He was constantly searching for a father who would never return. He spent a lot of time in counseling, sorting through this past. But the symbol of his liberation came the day he gave flowers for the sanctuary. His note for the bulletin simply said, "In honor of my father." When I read those words, I knew that he had finally forgiven his father. He had honored his past. Now he was free to move into the future.

To honor Father and Mother also means that we do not make them more than they were. They were neither devils nor gods. If we make them more than mortal, they will continue to govern our lives and determine our identity. So we must honor their humanity if we are ever to live as free adults. A time comes, according to Genesis, to leave our father and mother and cling to another (2:24). This is God's created order. Some of us leave by giving thanks to our parents; others leave by giving forgiveness. But we all have to leave. And we all have to turn to our heavenly Father to know who we are.

Those who have learned to receive their lives from God find it easier not just to honor their parents, but to revere all life as sacred because God creates it. And that brings us to the sixth commandment, which prohibits murder. Taking a human life is the ultimate rebellion against the Creator, for in doing so you assume sovereignty over life and death—a role that belongs to God alone.

Perhaps you are thinking that when it comes to this commandment, you can finally check the "not guilty" box. But then Jesus confronts you in his Sermon on the Mount: "You have heard that it was said . . . , 'You shall not murder.' . . . But I tell you that anyone who is angry with a brother or sister will be subject to judgment" (Matt. 5:21-22). For Jesus, righteousness is not a matter of what you avoid doing, but of what you do— even of what you think and feel.

Jesus is not giving us a new law. He is simply returning to the spirit of the Law of Moses (see Matt. 5:17-19). By the sixth commandment, God never meant that as long as you don't murder a person you hate, you're okay in God's eyes. He created the person you despise. So we dare not savor our anger. That will inevitably manifest itself in gossip or other diminishing activities that tarnish the sacred image stamped on a human life (Q&A 105).

One of the most redemptive things a Christian can do is to cherish the image of God embedded in ordinary people. Have you ever cuddled a baby and made a fool of yourself cooing just to get a little smile? Have you ever caught your spouse's eye across a crowded room, smiled, and winked? Have you ever held a wrinkled hand and listened to stories from long ago? Have you ever been the last one to leave a restaurant because you got carried away in conversation with a friend? Have you ever cried at a funeral for someone you are going to miss? Have you ever had to stop reading the news because you just couldn't bear it, or stared at a picture of a malnourished baby and started to pray? If your answer is no, the chances are good you've never revered life. And if that's true, the chances are good that you're already dead.

HONORING BOUNDARIES

When we come to the seventh and eighth commandments— "You shall not commit adultery" and "You shall not steal"—we discover the wonderful irony that freedom is found only within boundaries and limitations (see Q&A 108-111).

"You shall not" leaves no room for nuance or rationalization. How do we get around "You shall not"? As the old saying goes, what Moses brought down from Mount Sinai were not Ten Suggestions; they're Ten Commandments. It was so long ago that Moses came down the mountain with these commands written in stone by the finger of God. Since that day, how many empires have risen and fallen? How many generations have come and gone? And how many frontiers has society crossed? But the absolute truths of the commands persevere because they were written on our hearts.

It is difficult to believe that many people do not think adultery and stealing are wrong. If you are the type of person who breaks these commandments easily, the chances are good that you're not the type who reads books about sixteenth-century catechisms. But even when we know what is wrong, we still break the commandments more often than we think.

Those of us who have not committed the act of adultery are told by Jesus that we are just as guilty if we have lusted after someone (Matt. 5:27-28). That pretty much includes all of us. Jesus' main concern was always the heart, where evil thoughts are born (Matt. 15:19). So the catechism explains that the commandment against adultery includes "all unchaste actions, looks, talk, thoughts, or desires" (Q&A 109). Who is not guilty of that?

And those who do not think they're thieves need to remember that stealing involves more than breaking into someone's house and taking a television. Isn't it also stealing when we take time that belongs to our children and give it to our work, or take time from our work and give it to our children? Isn't it stealing when we take away someone's reputation with gossip, or take money that belongs to God and spend it securing our own lives?

The catechism places this eighth commandment in the positive by calling each of us to "do whatever I can for my neighbor's good" (Q&A 111). Again, this sounds like Jesus. How often can we say, "I have done whatever I can for my neighbor"? Jesus wants us to know that none of us can sustain our pretensions to righteousness based on the law. According to Jesus, we've all broken all the commandments.

COMPASSION AND CONVICTION

Some of us use the Ten Commandments to convict adulterers and thieves. These folks just want moral clarity and conviction. Others hear these commands and cower with shame and secrets. They echo the words of David: "My sin is always before me" (Ps. 51:3). Those who know that confession hope for the same compassion Jesus offered the woman caught in the act of adultery (John 8:1-11).

The gospel always comes to us with both compassion and conviction. "Neither do I condemn you," Jesus tells the woman. *Compassion.* "Go and sin no more," he concludes. *Conviction.* You understand only half the gospel if you just cling to one of those words.

Unfortunately the spiritual landscape of Christianity is littered with churches that offer only half a gospel, which is really no gospel at all. It is easy to be a church that stands for nothing but compassion. Those congregations say, "Whatever you believe is just fine, as long as you are sincere." But they do not preach a lot on the Ten Commandments or Jesus' interpretation of them.

It is also easy to be a church that stands for every conviction except compassion. Those congregations make you feel better about yourself by judging others. "Look out for them. They're sinners," we're told. But those churches have to edit out the many biblical texts that proclaim God's grace. To be a church that finds its life in Christ means we have the more difficult challenge of holding conviction and compassion together.

PURSUING TRUTH

The Ten Commandments begin with our relationship to God and conclude by directing our relationships with our neighbors. The ninth commandment directs us to tell the truth, and the tenth forbids us from coveting (see Q&A 112-113; Ex. 20:16-17). That's the way spiritual ethics always work: we demonstrate our relationship with God by our freedom to honor our neighbor.

One of the most interesting characters of the Bible is Pilate. He has done what it takes to rise to a position of relative importance in Rome's civil bureaucracy. By the time he encounters Jesus, it is apparent that he has made so many compromises with the system and with himself that he has lost his understanding of the truth. When he is tried before Pilate, Jesus says that he came into the world to bear witness to the truth (John 18:37). Pilate responds by asking, "What is truth?" (v. 38). The truth is a clouded memory for this successful bureaucrat.

What Pilate understood was expedience. Expedience had gotten him where he was in his profession, and expedience told him that freeing Jesus would do nothing for his career.

Pilate also understood ideology. The Romans defended their political position with the idea of *Pax Romana* ("Roman peace"), just as the Jewish Zealots defended their position with the idea of revolution. These ideologies led to constant conflict. Pilate knew that any injustice or abuse could always be explained away by ideology. But truth? What is truth?

If ever there were a question for our day, this is it. We also know about expedience. Like Pilate, we too have learned to do what it takes to get where we are. We don't think about whether our choices are true. We don't even know what that means. We worry only whether our choices are successful. And we also know about competing ideologies: Republican vs. Democrat, management vs. labor, majority vs. minority, and the list goes on. "But truth?" we echo; "What is truth?"

Even while Pilate was asking this question, he was staring right at the Truth. The church believes that Jesus is the way, the truth, and the life (John 14:6). This is not truth in the form of religious laws and moralism, which only digress into more ideology. Rather, it is truth as a person. Jesus Christ is the Truth because he is the revelation of God. He is the "God with us" who came to restore us to sacred communion by grace. That's the deepest truth we know. It's the center that holds together the Christian, the church, and the world. Everything else finds its truth by its proximity to the grace of a God with us all.

Jesus claimed that this truth has little to do with expediency for saving ourselves or with ideological commitments that only divide us. But the truth has everything to do with the witness we make about our neighbor. As the catechism instructs, our responsibility is not just to avoid lying about our neighbor, but also "to guard and advance my neighbor's good name" (Q&A 112). None of us have done enough of that.

One of our difficulties with the ninth commandment is that we have lost our understanding of who is our neighbor. We think our neighbors are the people who live next door to us, who are like us. But in the Bible our neighbor is any person in need of mercy.

Remember Jesus' parable of the Good Samaritan (Luke 10:29-37)? He tells the story in response to a lawyer who asks,

"What must I do to inherit eternal life?" As a typical rabbi, Jesus responds to the question by asking a question himself: "What does the law say?" The lawyer responds, "You shall love the Lord your God with all your heart, soul, strength, and mind—and your neighbor as yourself." Jesus says, in essence, "Well, there you go. Do this and you will live." But, trying to justify himself, the lawyer asks, "Ah, but who is my neighbor?" That's when Jesus begins the story: A man is jumped by robbers, who beat him up and leave him on the road. A priest walks by and does nothing. A Levite sees him and crosses the street to avoid the unpleasant scene. But a Samaritan, an outsider thought to be a sinner, takes care of the victim. Then Jesus asks, "Who do you think was a neighbor to the man who fell into the hands of robbers?"

Jesus has just turned the lawyer's question around. The real question isn't "Who is my neighbor?" The question is "Who is going to care for those in need?" The neighborhood of God is never established by similarity. It emerges only when we offer mercy.

That means that God's community stands over against the divided communities of our society that clump rich folks here and poor folks there, people of this color here and people of that color there, conservative religious people here and all the sinful Samaritans way over there, where they can't defile us. The neighborhood of God includes only one group of people: those in need of mercy.

In all the times I have been to the emergency room of a hospital, I have never, ever, heard anyone in agony on a stretcher look up at the physician and ask, "Now, are you a Republican?" When we're hurting, we don't care about our doctor's politics, color, or even religion. We just want someone to make the hurting stop. The core truth by which we live is that we all hurt, and that we all need the grace of God found in Jesus Christ. And to call ourselves Christians is to participate in Jesus' grace-offering ministry.

So to avoid being merciful—because it is not expedient or convenient, or because the person in need offends our ideology or morality—is to divide the neighborhood of God. It is to say that someone doesn't belong. And that is to bear false witness against our neighbor.

When Jesus commissioned his disciples, he sent them to Jerusalem, Judea, Samaria, and the ends of the earth to be true witnesses (Acts 1:8). The true witness stands against the false one by proclaiming that on the cross the Savior stretched out his arms wide enough to embrace the whole world with grace.

To be clear, when we say that God gives us grace, we are not saying God gives us what we want. Grace means that God gives us what we need. Sometimes what we need is freedom from the things we want. And that leads us to the tenth commandment: "You shall not covet . . . anything that belongs to your neighbor."

The catechism seems to give an odd interpretation to this commandment. Rather than commenting about coveting that new Audi or fine suburban home, it tells us "that not even the slightest desire or thought contrary to any one of God's commandments should ever arise in our hearts" (Q&A 113). Taking a very wide view, the catechism warns us that, ultimately, covetousness is the desire to live apart from God and outside the boundaries of his commandments.

This returns us to that great irony of life: true freedom is always found within limitations. That's what the commandments teach us. We live within boundaries. We cannot take something just because we want it. This lesson is as old as the Garden of Eden.

Like Adam and Eve, we are all placed in a garden that God has called good. There is much fruit in this garden that we can freely take, and many blessings within it that we can enjoy. But there is always something in the midst of it that is forbidden. We can see it. It is the one thing missing in the midst of our lives, and we think about it every day. But it is not ours for the taking. Unfortunately, we let it become the very thing we want most. We lose interest in the rest of the garden. But in reaching for the forbidden fruit, we lose the garden we had. And only then do we realize that the garden we had was paradise.

That doesn't mean we cannot make changes in our lives. It means we cannot assume that the whole world is ours for the taking. And it means we need to stop thinking about taking and start thinking about receiving. The positive way to say "You shall not covet" is to claim, "Find joy in what God is giving you."

There is always something behind our temptation to break the tether of the commandments. That is the quest for happiness. When we think happiness is not something we receive but something that comes from a quest, we are blind to the blessings we have and obsessed with taking what we can. We say that we were just desperate for love or that we were just angry that someone had more than we did—and when we saw the fruit that looked pleasing, we took it. But we never find happiness in things we take from others, whether it's intimacy or things or time. If you start out on the quest for happiness, you'll just keep consuming your whole life. That next thing or person will always be the idol that vainly promises happiness. And you will find that you have stolen your soul from God and enslaved it again. So it's not just a matter of whether others will miss the things you take. The big question is "What will it make of your soul if you become a taker?"

We covet different things. Some of us covet our neighbor's house or car or children. Others covet the achievements of our neighbors at work. Still others covet the wonderful relationships that others seem to have. What we all have in common is our tendency to go shopping for a life like our neighbor's. Nothing could be more enslaving.

There is no better way to lose your life than to keep measuring it by the standards of your neighbors. You will always come up short because someone else is always doing better. But those who pursue the truth are free from such small lives. They're done looking around at everyone else. They're done obsessing about getting a life like someone else. Now they are looking up. They are receiving the truth from God: we're all in need of mercy. Every person we envy is a living soul who needs mercy as much as we do.

"You will know the truth, and the truth will set you free" (John 8:32). God's great truth frees us from both the possessions and the judgments of our neighbors. And it frees us at last to love our neighbors. That's the only way to live in the neighborhood of God, the promised land where everyone lives in freedom.

CHAPTER SIX

TEACH US TO PRAY

(Q&A 116-129)

A forty-five-year-old man sits in his car. He's unsure how he made it home after leaving his doctor's office. The physician tried to be caring as she broke the news, but there is no way to anesthetize the diagnosis of terminal pancreatic cancer. He finds it odd that he's not thinking about what it means that he will die. What he can't figure out is how to explain the news to his wife and children. From someplace deep inside him, buried long ago during years of worship, emerges the urge to pray. He doesn't know how to approach God about this—what to say, exactly, or even if the prayer will do any good. He just knows he has to pray.

As the tears begin to slide down his cheeks, his hands squeeze the steering wheel. He bows his head and begins, "Dear God . . ." But that's as far as he can go.

WHY PRAY?

As our historians remind us, the world is always coming to an end. What they mean is that the life we have long known is about to change, as it always has. Whether we are studying civilizations and empires or our individual journeys through life, the discovery is always the same: there is an end to what we know. Christians believe that the cross of loss is the means of discovering more life than we have ever known. This is why we pray. We pray not just to be spared the inevitable losses of life for a while longer. Far more important, we pray to see that in life and death our lives belong to the God who promises us a future filled with hope.

The Heidelberg Catechism concludes with an extended section on prayer. This is surprising because we were expecting it to end like most sermons and confessional documents—with a call to mission. But this wondrous document of the Christian faith claims that in the end we find ourselves in prayer. And whether we realize it or not, our prayers are really about gratitude. Eventually it becomes clear that all we achieve and all we lose, including our lives, leads us to pray because prayer is the ultimate statement of the fact that we are not our own. We "belong—body and soul, in life and in death—to [our] faithful Savior, Jesus Christ" (Q&A 1). It is our only comfort.

So the catechism ends where it began—with comfort. But now the focus is on gratitude.

In the last chapter we explored how faithful obedience to God's law is an expression of gratitude for our freedom. Now, in prayer, we find the gratitude that motivates us to do all that is commanded of us as Christ's disciples. This is why the catechism states, "Prayer is the most important part of the thankfulness God requires of us" (Q&A 116).

Praying leaves us grateful not because it moves God to change the way things are, but because prayer places us in the proper relationship with God (Q&A 117). God is faithful and good, and we are needy. We all end up on our knees at some time or another, asking God to help us. And the catechism says that's precisely where we belong. We bring our concerns in life to God because we belong to this particular Savior, which means so do our concerns. But sometimes God answers, "No." Even then we are eventually made grateful because the very act of praying renews our holy relationship.

Often I am asked whether prayer works. What the person is really asking is Does it change things? And my response is always a resounding, "Yes!" But in my experience, mostly what prayer changes is the person who is praying. I firmly believe that God is active in the world and intervenes in our lives. But the heart of prayer is that we enter into communion with our God. And as we take our stand in that divine presence, we come to see that in life and death we have always been held in gracious and secure hands. That changes us from being anxious to grateful. And until we arrive at gratitude, we are not at the end of any journey through loss and grief. But without prayer we lose our way.

We are not asked to believe in prayer. We are asked to believe in the God to whom we pray (Q&A 116). If our belief were in our own prayers, we would remain anxious about the quality and careful construction of what we tell God—as if we could convince him to intervene if we just asked the right way.

As the catechism teaches, we should bring to God in prayer "everything we need, spiritually and physically" (Q&A 118). But God's response is never based on the eloquence of our prayers. Like the man who sits stunned in his car after learning that he will soon die, sometimes the most we can pray is, "Dear God . . . " When this happens, the Holy Spirit completes our prayers on our behalf (see Rom. 8:26-27). We are never on our own after starting with, "Dear God. . . . "

When I was a teenager, our well-meaning church youth group leaders taught us that all prayer should begin with *acknowledgment* of God's glory, then move to *confession* of our sins, followed by *thanksgiving* for all the blessings we've received. Only then should we finally get to *supplications,* asking for what we want God to do for us. Our leaders assured us that this must be the biblical way to pray, because the first letters of those four words spell ACTS—which is the fifth book of the New Testament. "There you have it," they said.

The great problem with that formula, of course, is that the Bible is filled with prayers that don't abide by those rules. The best prayers are found in the Psalms. Sometimes the psalmist focuses on lament from beginning to end. And at other times the prayer is all about petition or confession or thanksgiving. Since prayer is a way of renewing our relationship with God, like all lively relationships the communication cannot be reduced to formulas.

Formulas, prescriptions, and appropriateness are beside the point when it comes to prayer. The point of all prayer is to find ourselves in conversation with our gracious God. As we start to pay attention to this conversation, it turns into communion, and then we begin to care more about the communion than the thing we were praying about.

This communion with God is always carried on in the atmosphere of grace. That means there are no bad prayers and no good prayers. The new Christian or child who stumbles through prayer is just as compelling to the heart of God as the theologically trained pastor who invokes all three persons of the Trinity over the church potluck.

It's not about the prayer. It's always about the God to whom we pray. And renewing our communion with the holy God to whom we belong is always more comforting than receiving whatever it is we are asking for.

As we saw in chapter 1, when a little child skins a knee and runs to a parent's lap in tears, she is soon comforted by the parent who holds her and kisses her "boo boo." Before long the child is thinking more about being in the comforting lap of the parent than about her skinned knee. Love casts out fear (1 John 4:18). In prayer we move from our many anxieties to the overwhelming comfort of being in the lap of our heavenly Parent. Before long we scoot down off God's lap, grateful for the love we've received. And that gratitude emboldens us to return to the rough-and-tumble game of life.

So we need to stop thinking about "effective" prayers. Prayer isn't a leash on God that allows us to drag him to our own direction. Rather, it is an amazing opportunity to connect our hearts to God's own heart (Q&A 117). And when find ourselves in communion with the God who loves and listens, we are so overwhelmed by grace that we can only be grateful. That is always when we are at our best. That frees us to venture back into life unafraid. The perfect love we find in prayer casts out our fear. And only those who are free from anxiety can return to their mission in life. So in its own way, the catechism ends in mission after all.

THE LORD'S PRAYER

The catechism concludes with an exposition of the Lord's Prayer (Q&A 119)—not because it is the only prayer we should ever pray, but because it provides wonderful insights into the dynamics at work in all prayer. Not only that, but this is the prayer that Jesus gave to his disciples when they asked him to teach them how to pray (Q&A 118). So Christians around the globe, speaking most of the languages under the sun, gather together regularly to say this prayer. It is our way of rehearsing the act of praying that helps us understand all of our many other prayers, including the ones that cannot get past "Dear God. . . ."

Like all pastors, I am sometimes called to the emergency room late at night because a parishioner is in grave trouble. When I arrive, the person in crisis is usually sequestered under the care of the doctors and nurses. That means that most of my care initially focuses on the anxious family members who sit in the hospital's waiting room. I have always thought that this room is a powerful metaphor for all of life. It's amazing how much time we spend in waiting rooms of all sorts when a relationship, job, or future dream is in crisis. What will happen? Will we be okay, or is this the end? We don't know. We just have to wait and see.

What I have discovered over the years is that no one who is in the waiting room during an emergency is interested in creative theology. We just want to be reminded of what we already know; we want help in believing what we believe. We want to say things like the Lord's Prayer. That's how we find comfort.

C.S. Lewis reminded us that children love to have the same story told over and over, with the very same words.[12] If you try to change the story, a child will quickly interrupt to say, "That's not how it goes." He wants the same "surprise" of discovering that Little Red Riding Hood's grandmother was actually the mean wolf. It's easier to appreciate the twists in the story when you know they're coming. This frees us from being overwhelmed. We can cope with the wolves that suddenly appear because we know that in the end there is still a Happily Ever After.

Lewis also pointed out that the "unliterary man" reads a story only once, thinking that he is then done with it and can move on. Literary readers keep probing the same story in search of new insights. But they can do that only because they already know how the story ends.

That's also why some people return to a museum to gaze on the same painting or sculpture over and over, or why others buy copies of favorite films they love to watch more than once. They know this piece of art so well, but they cannot get enough of it.

And that's why Christians keep exploring the same biblical texts. It's not because we don't know the text. Rather, it is because we do. That's the attraction.

So it is with the Lord's Prayer. It's the one prayer most Christians have memorized. The last thing anyone wants is for the pastor to suggest a change in the wording. Even though variations do occur in the prayer among the different Christian traditions, everyone wants to say the version he or she learned as a child. This yearning rises from our souls. We need to say the same words over and over because they are trusted guides that invite us back into communion with our God.

PRAYING TO OUR FATHER

The catechism begins its exposition of the Lord's Prayer by claiming that the opening words "awaken in us . . . a childlike reverence and trust that through Christ God has become our Father" (Q&A 120). So all prayer is conducted as a family conversation. We come to God not as outsiders making claims about what

God should do, nor as beggars hoping for a handout, but as children already convinced of the Father's deep love for us.

To call God our Father is not to limit the Creator to a masculine gender. It is clear from the opening chapters of Genesis that both males and females are made in the image of God, who is the creative source of both. So the term *father* refers not to the being or identity of God. We call God our Father only because this is the language Jesus used to describe his own relationship to God—and through the Holy Spirit we have been drawn into their beloved relationship.

If Jesus had referred to God only as his parent, that would have left the relationship between them formal and unspecific. But Jesus ran into hot water with the religious leaders of his day because he refused to limit God to a theological otherness. He insisted on demonstrating intimacy with the Holy One who is with us.

The word Jesus used for *father* in the Aramaic is "Abba," which has the connotation of "Daddy." The point of praying "Our Father" is that God is not a concept, but a Person we know in an intimate relationship. You can climb into the lap of a Daddy. He goes to your ballet and piano recitals. He cheers for you in the stands when you play football. He is waiting when you get home too late from a date. And he is always eager to talk with you. But your heavenly Father also sets the rules, establishes the boundaries, and most important, gives you his family name—so you always know who you are.

The danger of referring to God as our Father is that many people have had earthly fathers who were deeply flawed in their ability to love. Some suggest that makes it impossible to use the language of "Father" in addressing God—because the word is laden with so many memories of hurt. But it is also possible to see God as the redemptive image of what a father is supposed to be and do.

My own father got in his car one day and abandoned us when I was sixteen years old. I didn't see him again until thirty years later, when I spoke at his funeral. It would be impossible to explain how much heartache that created. I could have rejected the whole notion of thinking of God as my Father. But somewhere along the way I chose to rejoice that I had a heavenly Father who would never leave or forsake me. And that has made all the difference in my own understanding of how to be a father to my children.

The Lord's Prayer reminds us that this is our Father "in heaven." That is not to remove God from us, but to remind us that God is the perfect Father. And the grace of this for all earthly fathers is that we don't have to be perfect. Instead, our mission is to raise our children with the realization that they have a heavenly Father who is always faithful. He is more involved with the concerns of their lives than we can even see.

By instructing us to pray to "our Father," Jesus reminds us that God has more than one child. We cannot understand ourselves without remembering that we have siblings in the household of God. Most of these siblings have gone before us. My faith is shaped and molded by those who have already faced every trial I could possibly encounter. And I receive their great faith as my inheritance.

Some of our brothers and sisters live today in conditions that are severe. Abba Father has been quite clear about how we are expected to care for these siblings. So when we hear about Christians being persecuted in places like Sudan, we cannot think of that as a distant international problem. Our brothers and sisters are suffering. Thus, even the beginning of the Lord's Prayer is missional. We always pray as one of God's many children, and through the act of praying we are made grateful for our siblings in the faith. Nothing is more transformative for *my* problems as lifting my eyes to see *our* problems—and the Father who is actively involved in all our lives.

FAMILY TALK

As the catechism notes, the first petition of the Lord's Prayer is that God's name be "hallowed," or "made holy." We tend not to think of this as a petition, because we assume petitions are about what we need God to do for us. But the catechism helpfully explains that we honor the holy name of God through "all our living—what we think, say, and do" (Q&A 122).

So the phrase "Hallowed be your name" is actually not about God, who is holy whether we affirm that or not. We pray those words to ask that our lives as Christians would reflect the holiness of the God to whom we belong.

That's asking a lot. We know ourselves—our limitations, failures, and the sins to which we are addicted. How can we ever live up to the expectation of reflecting God's holiness? But remember, we are not asking ourselves to be more holy. We're asking for this grace from God, who does for us what we cannot do for ourselves.

That brings us back to gratitude once again. The burden is not on our shoulders to demonstrate our thankfulness by being holy on our own. Rather, we are grateful that the Spirit continues to work through us to reveal God's holiness in our lives despite our tendency to be anything but holy. Even our many failures in righteousness reveal the holiness of a God who forgives our sin and frees us to "think, say, and do" that which reflects our communion with the Savior.

In the worship traditions of the Old Testament, the holiness of God was particularly associated with the Holy of Holies in the temple. A large, heavy veil separated the Holy of Holies from the rest of the world. Once a year the high priest would venture behind it to offer a sacrifice for the sins of the people. It was such a frightening experience to encounter the holy God that the other priests would tie a rope around the high priest's ankle so they could drag him out of the Holy of Holies in case he was smitten by God's judgment. But the very moment the judgment of God was satisfied on the cross of Jesus Christ, the veil was ripped apart from the top, which made it clear that was God's own doing. It was heaven's proclamation that the holiness of God would never again be confined to a particular piece of religious real estate. Now it flows into every corner of the world and every human heart that God reclaims as his own.

For that reason the Bible knows nothing of our contemporary distinction between the sacred and the secular. It's all sacred. After the atonement of Jesus Christ, the distinction is between the sacred and the profane. We can profane words, money, sex, and our holy lives by using them for a purpose other than expressing gratitude to God. But we cannot remove their inherent holy status by relegating them to a realm we call secular.

As Jesus Christ demonstrated, the holiness of God is not contaminated by its association with sinners. Jesus was often found in the company of sinners, which offended those who thought of themselves as righteous. But as Jesus kept explaining, only those who realize that they need a Savior are brought back home to our Father.

Nowhere is this more vividly illustrated than in Jesus' parable of the prodigal son (Luke 15:11-32). By the time we get to the end of this story, we realize that the point is not to be as righteous as the careful elder brother who followed the rules, but to find ourselves in the forgiving arms of the father.

The parable ends with the father pleading for his elder son to join the celebration for the return of the prodigal. But we do not know whether the elder brother will actually do so. The story is left open so we supposedly righteous children can complete it by deciding if we will set aside our own efforts at being holy and run into the outstretched arms of our Father. There is no other way to be holy.

YOUR KINGDOM COME

The second petition in the Lord's Prayer is "Your kingdom come," and the third is "Your will be done, on earth as it is in heaven." They're closely related. To pray for the kingdom of God to come is to ask that Jesus Christ and the Holy Spirit will rule our lives "more and more" (Q&A 123). To pray for God's will to be done on earth as it is in heaven is to ask for the transformation of our own wills so that we may "carry out the work we are called to" (Q&A 124).

In other words, we are praying for the will to participate in the unfolding of God's future for the world, including our little corner of it.

When we pray for the kingdom of God to come, we are already acknowledging that the present will not last. We're bowing our heads to say, "I will not make the present absolute or take it too seriously. I will not base my decisions on the present order of a society that shows me how to manipulate the economic system to my benefit. Since the majority of the world lives in poverty, I will not stay silent just because I am doing okay."

The present tense is vanquished every time we pray the Lord's Prayer. We acknowledge that God has already determined the future of the world, that this future is coming, and that the only issue left for me is to ask that God conform my will to his own—that someday it will be done on earth as it already is in heaven.

When you're reading a mystery novel, the suspense is sometimes so overwhelming that you can't resist peeking at the end of the story. This is exactly why God gave us the book of Revelation. When we read its final chapters, we discover that in the end we will find God making his home among mortals. We will live in a new city with a river of life flowing through it. And out of that river stands a tree whose leaves are for the healing of the nations (Rev. 21:1-4; 22:1-5). It's a great ending. It gets a little scary just before then, but the very end of the story could not be more promising.

The point of God revealing this glorious ending is not just that it gives us a glimpse of the new kingdom that's coming. It also renews our vision of our mission today. That mission is to watch for signs that the future kingdom is breaking into the present, and then to throw ourselves into preparing its way. This new kingdom doesn't spread from our hearts out into the waiting world; rather, it spreads from God's established future into our hearts. There's no doubt about the future. The Holy Spirit has already written it down in Scripture. What is in question is our response today.

As beloved children of the heavenly Father, we pray for insight as to how we may best participate in our family business of seeking the new kingdom that is coming.

OUR DAILY BREAD

It's only in the fourth petition that the Lord's Prayer gets around to the kinds of things we usually associate with prayer—our needs. And the first thing we ask for is "our daily bread." The catechism makes it clear that we ask the Savior to "take care of all our physical needs so that we come to know that [God is] the only source of everything good" (Q&A 125).

All the ordinary blessings of life come from above. The beauty of the winter's fresh snow, the constantly returning spring tulips, the family dinner table filled with food and laughter, the tender smell of a newborn baby, the comfort two old men find in playing chess in the park, the excitement of watching a runner break the tape of the finish line, the first time two teenagers hold hands—everything good comes from God. It's bread for our souls.

The soul can handle the crises of life as long as the bread that comes from heaven has nourished it. But God gives us this bread not by keeping the scales of problems and blessings even. The purpose of everything God gives us, even the gifts we don't want, is to draw us back to the heavenly Father in prayer.

When the Hebrews were making their way through the wilderness after leaving Egypt, God fed them with manna to keep them alive along the way. The manna was a sort of bread that rained down from heaven every morning. It wasn't much. But it was their daily bread. It came with a couple of instructions: everyone had to gather his or her own, and they had to gather it every day. Both are wonderful metaphors for how we receive the care God offers each day. Every morning the attentive person will remember that God has already provided everything necessary for life: the sun above us, the Earth that spun on its axis to give us another day, the breath in our lungs, the food we will eat. And everything that we cherish in life—our most important relationships, gifts for service, our health, and certainly our restored relationship to God—has come not as a goal to be achieved, but a daily blessing to receive.

In addition to the concrete realities of God's blessings, manna also provides a helpful metaphor for how we grow in our faith in God. *Manna* in the Hebrew means, "What is it?" So every day the people would gather up their family's daily ration of "What is it." I am sure they then prepared it as creatively as they could. But when they placed it on the family table, their children no doubt asked, "What is it?"

God kept his people alive on the journey with a critical question: "What is it, God, that you are doing? What is it that is so special about the promised land? What is it that you are making of us along the way?"

This question persevered for centuries until Jesus claimed that he was the new manna sent from God (John 6:51). By identifying himself with the manna, Jesus was essentially saying that he is the new "What is it?" So the answer to our old question is also a question, but it is a better question. And finding better questions is at least half of the agenda in Christian spirituality. Now the real question is "What is it that Jesus the Savior is doing?" As we take in that question every day, our souls are nourished—even if we don't have the faintest clue about the answer. The nourishment comes not from answers, but from focusing on the work of the Savior. Even asking the question feeds our souls, because what we long for is not clarity but the God to whom we belong.

The catechism goes on to explain that our confidence for having our needs met cannot come from our work, our worry, or from any creature (Q&A 125). Only the God we know in Jesus Christ meets our needs. So the daily bread we ask for is not just more of God's abundant blessings in life. It's also the prayerful reminder that we depend on the heavenly Father who through Jesus Christ provides for us even when we have more questions than answers. The grace is that we get to ask the questions to God, and that we don't have to provide our own insufficient responses.

FLOWING FORGIVENESS

The fifth petition of the Lord's Prayer bids us to pray, "Forgive us our debts, as we also have forgiven our debtors." As the catechism explains, this means that the atoning sacrifice of Jesus Christ not only frees us from the sin and evil that cling to us; it also gives us the power to forgive our neighbors (Q&A 126).

Our heavenly Father not only forgives our sins and frees us from our addictions; he also pours so much grace into our hearts that it overflows into our relationships with those around us. As the old saying goes, we cannot give what we have not first received. But from God we have received grace upon grace—enough to let it flow.

We learn to pray for this grace by reciting the Lord's Prayer day after day, week after week, year after year. The constant re-praying of these lines opens our eyes to the abundant power of forgiveness. Any broken relationship can be repaired no matter how much hurt is scattered around, but that will never happen without forgiving grace. And as this prayer teaches us, the only way we will find either the will or the courage to offer such forgiveness is by remembering that God has already forgiven us. He did that not just to free us from our debt to him, but also to free us to participate in his ministry of grace to the world around us. Forgiving is just another part of the family business of God.

We forgive those who hurt us not only for the sake of free-ing them from the judgment they deserve. We also forgive them for the sake of our own souls. As long as we remain angry and judgmental, we maintain distance not only from the sinner who hurt us, but from God. Ironically, that makes us sinners, since sin is anything that distances us from God. At the cross of Jesus Christ it became clear that God is intent on forgiving all who have sinned and fallen short of the glory of God (Rom. 3:23). So to be fully alive in Christ can only mean to participate in Christ's ongoing mission to forgive sins. If we refuse to fulfill this calling, that does not prevent the offender from being for-given by God. It just keeps us at a distance from God.

The ethicist Lewis Smedes wrote that to forgive is to set a prisoner free. And after we forgive, we discover that we were the prisoner. But this is hard. So we pray to find our own freedom through forgiving.

RESCUE US FROM EVIL

The sixth petition of the Lord's Prayer asks, "And do not bring us to the time of trial, but rescue us from the evil one."* This line of the prayer assumes that we are aware that evil exists. We ignore it to our peril.

From the time that Cain rose up against Abel, the world has been divided between those who do the hurting and those who are hurt, between the oppressor and the victim, between the unjust and the just. And beneath that lies a pervasive, devilish evil. But the catechism prevents us from externalizing this evil, as if everything bad that happens is the fault only of an otherworldly, malevolent power.

Instead, the catechism lists our sworn enemies as "the devil, the world, and our own flesh" (Q&A 127). So it isn't just the devil we have to worry about.

---

*Many Christians are familiar with another translation of this petition: "Lead us not into temptation, but deliver us from evil." As different as they seem, they mean essentially the same thing. This translation is from the New Revised Standard Version, which is used throughout the catechism. It should be noted that most scholars agree that the Greek here means "testing" more than "tempting," which we often associate with attraction to sin.

When the catechism calls the world our sworn enemy, it is referring to the economic and social coping devices we have developed for our prodigal lives, so far removed from the Father's house. North American society and economics are largely based on consumption. Therefore, the messages we receive continually urge us toward getting more. We hear ridiculous things like "Yes, you are not using your life to make a difference, but maybe you can find just as much joy if you buy a new boat." If a boat isn't all that tempting, there is always some other approach the world has for anesthetizing the pain of living without holy purpose.

Society claims that there are Haves and Have-Nots, and you need to do whatever you can to be one of the Haves. But when do we ever have enough? That's not the world God created. So we pray constantly to resist its temptations that addict us to yearning for more.

Our own flesh, the catechism reminds us, can also be our sworn enemy. God created the flesh and called it good, and in the incarnation of Jesus it was redeemed as holy again. But we can easily profane the flesh by allowing its desires to become our true god. The flesh is constantly hungry for more food, sex, happiness, and esteem—more of everything. But those hungers veil our deepest desire, which is for God. Yes, we are always hungry. Most of all, however, we hunger for God. As has been clear since the Garden of Eden, we flirt with evil when we allow the flesh to drive our lives away from God—when we reach for more than we were created to have. So we pray for the strength to control ourselves.

Every day we confront the evil that seeks to pull us away from God's holy kingdom. As the catechism teaches, we are engaged in a great spiritual struggle, which means we have to take a side in the battle (Q&A 127). What will it be for you: holiness or evil? No one can stay neutral. We all must decide if we will participate in God's holy kingdom that is coming, or if we will be enemies of that kingdom. That decision informs most every other choice in life.

DOXOLOGY

The Lord's Prayer concludes, "For the kingdom and the power and the glory are yours forever. Amen." This is also the fitting conclusion of the Heidelberg Catechism, and the best conclusion any of us can have for our lives.

Notice the all-important words "are yours." The Lord's Prayer teaches us to pray that whatever we accomplish and whatever failures we are tempted to hide "are yours, Almighty God." We leave it all to the Savior. Our lives were never supposed to be about the inevitably small kingdoms of straw we build for ourselves at home and in the workplace, or our own power to secure them, or the tinseled glory that comes with our insignificant victories. God cherishes us too much to let that be our meager end.

Instead, as people who belong to Jesus Christ, our lives have been caught up in God's great world-changing drama called redemption. We can never be more than a fleeting chapter of that drama, but the holy drama gives meaning to every chapter, no matter how short.

Usually we do not see that until we are gathered at a funeral for a person we love. In my line of work, I find myself at many of these services. My favorite part of funerals are the eulogies, when family and friends stand to speak about the deceased. After listening to eulogies for more than thirty years, it occurs to me that no one has ever stood to read the resume of the person who died or revealed how much money he or she left behind or held up that person's trophies.

No, in the end we just want to hear if this person's years were well lived—and about the glimpses of heaven we received through a life that was committed to something wonderful.

Eulogies are the great "Amen" to our lives. So before someone stands up to talk about us at our funerals, the catechism urges each of us to pray for the wisdom and courage to live as a person who knows "that I am not my own, but belong—body and soul, in life and in death—to my faithful Savior, Jesus Christ."

THE HEIDELBERG
CATECHISM

Perhaps the most well-known and widely used of the Reformation catechisms, the Heidelberg Catechism has been admired for its clarity as an expression of the Reformed faith, but especially for its warm and personal tone. Many of its questions and answers, especially Q&A 1, have been memorized by thousands and have became an anchor for faith. In 2013 we celebrate the 450th anniversary of this classic and beloved catechism.

This 450th Anniversary Edition of the Heidelberg Catechism (completed in 2011) is a fresh and accurate translation from the original German and Latin, using the 1988 translation of the Christian Reformed Church in North America as an English language base. It is also an ecumenical effort in that it is now the officially recognized translation of the Christian Reformed Church, the Presbyterian Church (USA), and the Reformed Church in America. This fits the original purpose of the catechism, which was not only to teach the faith, but also to unite various church factions in the German Palatinate in a common confession.

Most of the footnoted biblical references in this translation of the catechism were included in the early German and Latin editions, but the precise selection was approved by Synod 1975 of the Christian Reformed Church.

We thank the following people for their important and faithful work on the joint translation committee:

Lyle Bierma (Calvin Theological Seminary)
J. Todd Billings (Western Theological Seminary)
Dawn Devries (Union Presbyterian Seminary)
Eugene Heideman (Western Theological Seminary, Emeritus)
David Stubbs (Western Theological Seminary)
Leonard J. Vander Zee (CRC staff)
Charles White (RCA staff)

Note that Scripture quotations throughout the catechism, including the Lord's Prayer, are from the New Revised Standard Version of the Bible.

1 Q. **What is your only comfort
in life and in death?**

A. That I am not my own,[1]
but belong—
body and soul,
in life and in death—[2]
to my faithful Savior, Jesus Christ.[3]

He has fully paid for all my sins with his precious blood,[4]
and has set me free from the tyranny of the devil.[5]
He also watches over me in such a way[6]
that not a hair can fall from my head
without the will of my Father in heaven;[7]
in fact, all things must work together for my salvation.[8]

Because I belong to him,
Christ, by his Holy Spirit,
assures me of eternal life[9]
and makes me wholeheartedly willing and ready
from now on to live for him.[10]

[1] 1 Cor. 6:19-20
[2] Rom. 14:7-9
[3] 1 Cor. 3:23; Titus 2:14
[4] 1 Pet. 1:18-19; 1 John 1:7-9; 2:2
[5] John 8:34-36; Heb. 2:14-15; 1 John 3:1-11
[6] John 6:39-40; 10:27-30; 2 Thess. 3:3; 1 Pet. 1:5
[7] Matt. 10:29-31; Luke 21:16-18
[8] Rom. 8:28
[9] Rom. 8:15-16; 2 Cor. 1:21-22; 5:5; Eph. 1:13-14
[10] Rom. 8:1-17

2   **Q.**   **What must you know to**
          live and die in the joy of this comfort?

      A.   Three things:

             first, how great my sin and misery are;[1]

             second, how I am set free from all my sins and misery;[2]

             third, how I am to thank God for such deliverance.[3]

[1] Rom. 3:9-10; 1 John 1:10
[2] John 17:3; Acts 4:12; 10:43
[3] Matt. 5:16; Rom. 6:13; Eph. 5:8-10; 2 Tim. 2:15; 1 Pet. 2:9-10

Part I: Misery

LORD'S DAY 2

3   **Q.**   **How do you come to know your misery?**

      A.   The law of God tells me.[1]

[1] Rom. 3:20; 7:7-25

4   **Q.**   **What does God's law require of us?**

      A.   Christ teaches us this in summary in Matthew 22:37-40:

          "'You shall love the Lord your God

          with all your heart,

          and with all your soul,

          and with all your mind.'[1]

          This is the greatest and first commandment.

          "And a second is like it:

          'You shall love your neighbor as yourself.'[2]

          "On these two commandments hang

          all the law and the prophets."

[1] Deut. 6:5
[2] Lev. 19:18

5   **Q. Can you live up to all this perfectly?**

     A. No.[1]

        I have a natural tendency
        to hate God and my neighbor.[2]

[1] Rom. 3:9-20, 23; 1 John 1:8, 10
[2] Gen. 6:5; Jer. 17:9; Rom. 7:23-24; 8:7; Eph. 2:1-3; Titus 3:3

LORD'S DAY 3

6   **Q. Did God create people
       so wicked and perverse?**

     A. No.

        God created them good[1] and in his own image,[2]
          that is, in true righteousness and holiness,[3]
        so that they might
          truly know God their creator,[4]
          love him with all their heart,
          and live with God in eternal happiness,
        to praise and glorify him.[5]

[1] Gen. 1:31
[2] Gen. 1:26-27
[3] Eph. 4:24
[4] Col. 3:10
[5] Ps. 8

7   **Q. Then where does this corrupt human nature come from?**

     A. The fall and disobedience of our first parents,
          Adam and Eve, in Paradise.[1]
        This fall has so poisoned our nature[2]
          that we are all conceived and born
          in a sinful condition.[3]

[1] Gen. 3
[2] Rom. 5:12, 18-19
[3] Ps. 51:5

8   **Q.**   **But are we so corrupt**
           that we are totally unable to do any good
           and inclined toward all evil?

      A.   Yes,[1] unless we are born again
           by the Spirit of God.[2]

[1] Gen. 6:5; 8:21; Job 14:4; Isa. 53:6
[2] John 3:3-5

LORD'S DAY 4

9   **Q.**   **But doesn't God do us an injustice**
           by requiring in his law
           what we are unable to do?

      A.   No, God created human beings with the ability to keep the law.[1]
           They, however, provoked by the devil,[2]
              in willful disobedience,[3]
              robbed themselves and all their descendants of these gifts.[4]

[1] Gen. 1:31; Eph. 4:24
[2] Gen. 3:13; John 8:44
[3] Gen. 3:6
[4] Rom. 5:12, 18, 19

**10 Q. Does God permit
such disobedience and rebellion
to go unpunished?**

A. Certainly not.
God is terribly angry
with the sin we are born with
as well as the sins we personally commit.

As a just judge,
God will punish them both now and in eternity,[1]
having declared:
"Cursed is everyone who does not observe and obey
all the things written in the book of the law."[2]

[1] Ex. 34:7; Ps. 5:4-6; Nah. 1:2; Rom. 1:18; Eph. 5:6; Heb. 9:27
[2] Gal. 3:10; Deut. 27:26

11 Q. But isn't God also merciful?

A. God is certainly merciful,[1]
but also just.[2]
God's justice demands
that sin, committed against his supreme majesty,
be punished with the supreme penalty—
eternal punishment of body and soul.[3]

[1] Ex. 34:6-7; Ps. 103:8-9
[2] Ex. 34:7; Deut. 7:9-11; Ps. 5:4-6; Heb. 10:30-31
[3] Matt. 25:35-46

LORD'S DAY 5

12 Q. **According to God's righteous judgment**
   we deserve punishment
   both now and in eternity:
   how then can we escape this punishment
   and return to God's favor?

   A. God requires that his justice be satisfied.[1]
      Therefore the claims of this justice
      must be paid in full,
      either by ourselves or by another.[2]

[1] Ex. 23:7; Rom. 2:1-11
[2] Isa. 53:11; Rom. 8:3-4

13 Q. **Can we make this payment ourselves?**

   A. Certainly not.
      Actually, we increase our debt every day.[1]

[1] Matt. 6:12; Rom. 2:4-5

14 Q. **Can another creature—any at all—**
   pay this debt for us?

   A. No.
      To begin with,
         God will not punish any other creature
         for what a human is guilty of.[1]
      Furthermore,
         no mere creature can bear the weight
         of God's eternal wrath against sin
         and deliver others from it.[2]

[1] Ezek. 18:4, 20; Heb. 2:14-18
[2] Ps. 49:7-9; 130:3

**15 Q. What kind of mediator and deliverer
should we look for then?**

A. One who is a true[1] and righteous[2] human,
yet more powerful than all creatures,
that is, one who is also true God.[3]

[1] Rom. 1:3; 1 Cor. 15:21; Heb. 2:17
[2] Isa. 53:9; 2 Cor. 5:21; Heb. 7:26
[3] Isa. 7:14; 9:6; Jer. 23:6; John 1:1

LORD'S DAY 6

16 Q. Why must the mediator be a true and righteous human?

A. God's justice demands
that human nature, which has sinned,
must pay for sin;[1]
but a sinful human could never pay for others.[2]

[1] Rom. 5:12, 15; 1 Cor. 15:21; Heb. 2:14-16
[2] Heb. 7:26-27; 1 Pet. 3:18

17 Q. Why must the mediator also be true God?

A. So that the mediator,
by the power of his divinity,
might bear the weight of God's wrath in his humanity
and earn for us
and restore to us
righteousness and life.[1]

[1] Isa. 53; John 3:16; 2 Cor. 5:21

**18 Q. Then who is this mediator—
true God and at the same time
a true and righteous human?**

   A. Our Lord Jesus Christ,[1]
who was given to us
to completely deliver us
and make us right with God.[2]

[1] Matt. 1:21-23; Luke 2:11; 1 Tim. 2:5
[2] 1 Cor. 1:30

19 Q. How do you come to know this?

   A. The holy gospel tells me.
God began to reveal the gospel already in Paradise;[1]
later God proclaimed it
by the holy patriarchs[2] and prophets[3]
and foreshadowed it
by the sacrifices and other ceremonies of the law;[4]
and finally God fulfilled it
through his own beloved Son.[5]

[1] Gen. 3:15
[2] Gen. 22:18; 49:10
[3] Isa. 53; Jer. 23:5-6; Mic. 7:18-20; Acts 10:43; Heb. 1:1-2
[4] Lev. 1-7; John 5:46; Heb. 10:1-10
[5] Rom. 10:4; Gal. 4:4-5; Col. 2:17

20 Q. Are all people then saved through Christ just as they were lost through Adam?

A. No.
Only those are saved
who through true faith
are grafted into Christ
and accept all his benefits.[1]

[1] Matt. 7:14; John 3:16, 18, 36; Rom. 11:16-21

21 Q. What is true faith?

A. True faith is
not only a sure knowledge by which I hold as true
all that God has revealed to us in Scripture;[1]
it is also a wholehearted trust,[2]
which the Holy Spirit creates in me[3] by the gospel,[4]
that God has freely granted,
not only to others but to me also,[5]
forgiveness of sins,
eternal righteousness,
and salvation.[6]
These are gifts of sheer grace,
granted solely by Christ's merit.[7]

[1] John 17:3, 17; Heb. 11:1-3; James 2:19
[2] Rom. 4:18-21; 5:1; 10:10; Heb. 4:14-16
[3] Matt. 16:15-17; John 3:5; Acts 16:14
[4] Rom. 1:16; 10:17; 1 Cor. 1:21
[5] Gal. 2:20
[6] Rom. 1:17; Heb. 10:10
[7] Rom. 3:21-26; Gal. 2:16; Eph. 2:8-10

22 Q. What then must a Christian believe?

A. All that is promised us in the gospel,[1]
a summary of which is taught us
in the articles of our universal
and undisputed Christian faith.

[1] Matt. 28:18-20; John 20:30-31

23 Q. What are these articles?

A. I believe in God, the Father almighty,
creator of heaven and earth.

I believe in Jesus Christ, his only begotten Son, our Lord,
who was conceived by the Holy Spirit
and born of the virgin Mary.
He suffered under Pontius Pilate,
was crucified, died, and was buried;
he descended to hell.
The third day he rose again from the dead.
He ascended to heaven
and is seated at the right hand of God the Father almighty.
From there he will come to judge the living and the dead.

I believe in the Holy Spirit,
the holy catholic church,
the communion of saints,
the forgiveness of sins,
the resurrection of the body,
and the life everlasting. Amen.

LORD'S DAY 8

24 Q. How are these articles divided?

A. Into three parts:
> God the Father and our creation;
> God the Son and our deliverance;
> and God the Holy Spirit and our sanctification.

**25 Q. Since there is only one divine being,[1]
why do you speak of three:
Father, Son, and Holy Spirit?**

A. Because that is how
> God has revealed himself in his Word:[2]
> these three distinct persons
> are one, true, eternal God.

[1] Deut. 6:4; 1 Cor. 8:4, 6
[2] Matt. 3:16-17; 28:18-19; Luke 4:18 (Isa. 61:1); John 14:26; 15:26; 2 Cor. 13:14; Gal. 4:6; Tit. 3:5-6

LORD'S DAY 9

26 Q. **What do you believe when you say,
"I believe in God, the Father almighty,
creator of heaven and earth"?**

A. That the eternal Father of our Lord Jesus Christ,
who out of nothing created heaven and earth
and everything in them,[1]
who still upholds and rules them
by his eternal counsel and providence,[2]
is my God and Father
because of Christ the Son.[3]

I trust God so much that I do not doubt
he will provide
whatever I need
for body and soul,[4]
and will turn to my good
whatever adversity he sends upon me
in this sad world.[5]

God is able to do this because he is almighty God[6]
and desires to do this because he is a faithful Father.[7]

[1] Gen. 1-2; Ex. 20:11; Ps. 33:6; Isa. 44:24; Acts 4:24; 14:15
[2] Ps. 104; Matt. 6:30; 10:29; Eph. 1:11
[3] John 1:12-13; Rom. 8:15-16; Gal. 4:4-7; Eph. 1:5
[4] Ps. 55:22; Matt. 6:25-26; Luke 12:22-31
[5] Rom. 8:28
[6] Gen. 18:14; Rom. 8:31-39
[7] Matt. 7:9-11

LORD'S DAY 10

27 Q. **What do you understand
by the providence of God?**

A. The almighty and ever present power of God[1]
by which God upholds, as with his hand,
heaven
and earth
and all creatures,[2]
and so rules them that
leaf and blade,
rain and drought,
fruitful and lean years,
food and drink,
health and sickness,
prosperity and poverty—[3]
all things, in fact,
come to us
not by chance[4]
but by his fatherly hand.[5]

[1] Jer. 23:23-24; Acts 17:24-28
[2] Heb. 1:3
[3] Jer. 5:24; Acts 14:15-17; John 9:3; Prov. 22:2
[4] Prov. 16:33
[5] Matt. 10:29

**28 Q. How does the knowledge
of God's creation and providence help us?**

A. We can be patient when things go against us,[1]
thankful when things go well,[2]
and for the future we can have
good confidence in our faithful God and Father
that nothing in creation will separate us from his love.[3]
For all creatures are so completely in God's hand
that without his will
they can neither move nor be moved.[4]

[1] Job 1:21-22; James 1:3
[2] Deut. 8:10; 1 Thess. 5:18
[3] Ps. 55:22; Rom. 5:3-5; 8:38-39
[4] Job 1:12; 2:6; Prov. 21:1; Acts 17:24-28

God the Son

LORD'S DAY 11

**29 Q. Why is the Son of God called "Jesus,"
meaning "savior"?**

A. Because he saves us from our sins,[1]
and because salvation should not be sought
and cannot be found in anyone else.[2]

[1] Matt. 1:21; Heb. 7:25
[2] Isa. 43:11; John 15:5; Acts 4:11-12; 1 Tim. 2:5

30 Q. **Do those who look for
their salvation in saints,
in themselves, or elsewhere
really believe in the only savior Jesus?**

A. No.
Although they boast of being his,
by their actions they deny
the only savior, Jesus.[1]

Either Jesus is not a perfect savior,
or those who in true faith accept this savior
have in him all they need for their salvation.[2]

[1] 1 Cor. 1:12-13; Gal. 5:4
[2] Col. 1:19-20; 2:10; 1 John 1:7

LORD'S DAY 12

31 Q. **Why is he called "Christ,"
meaning "anointed"?**

A. Because he has been ordained by God the Father
and has been anointed with the Holy Spirit[1]
to be
our chief prophet and teacher[2]
who fully reveals to us
the secret counsel and will of God concerning our
deliverance;[3]
our only high priest[4]
who has delivered us by the one sacrifice of his body,[5]
and who continually pleads our cause with the Father;[6]

and our eternal king[7]
> who governs us by his Word and Spirit,
> and who guards us and keeps us
> in the freedom he has won for us.[8]

[1] Luke 3:21-22; 4:14-19 (Isa. 61:1); Heb. 1:9 (Ps. 45:7)
[2] Acts 3:22 (Deut. 18:15)
[3] John 1:18; 15:15
[4] Heb. 7:17 (Ps. 110:4)
[5] Heb. 9:12; 10:11-14
[6] Rom. 8:34; Heb. 9:24
[7] Matt. 21:5 (Zech. 9:9)
[8] Matt. 28:18-20; John 10:28; Rev. 12:10-11

32 Q. But why are you called a Christian?

A. Because by faith I am a member of Christ[1]
> and so I share in his anointing.[2]
>> I am anointed
>> to confess his name,[3]
>> to present myself to him as a living sacrifice of thanks,[4]
>> to strive with a free conscience against sin and the devil
>> in this life,[5]
>> and afterward to reign with Christ
>>> over all creation
>>> for eternity.[6]

[1] 1 Cor. 12:12-27
[2] Acts 2:17 (Joel 2:28); 1 John 2:27
[3] Matt. 10:32; Rom. 10:9-10; Heb. 13:15
[4] Rom. 12:1; 1 Pet. 2:5, 9
[5] Gal. 5:16-17; Eph. 6:11; 1 Tim. 1:18-19
[6] Matt. 25:34; 2 Tim. 2:12

33 Q. **Why is he called God's "only begotten Son"
when we also are God's children?**

    A. Because Christ alone is the eternal, natural Son of God.[1]
       We, however, are adopted children of God—
          adopted by grace through Christ.[2]

[1] John 1:1-3, 14, 18; Heb. 1
[2] John 1:12; Rom. 8:14-17; Eph. 1:5-6

34 Q. **Why do you call him "our Lord"?**

    A. Because—

        not with gold or silver,
         but with his precious blood—[1]
      he has set us free
         from sin and from the tyranny of the devil,[2]
      and has bought us,
         body and soul,
      to be his very own.[3]

[1] 1 Pet. 1:18-19
[2] Col. 1:13-14; Heb. 2:14-15
[3] 1 Cor. 6:20; 1 Tim. 2:5-6

35 Q. **What does it mean that he**
"was conceived by the Holy Spirit
and born of the virgin Mary"?

A. That the eternal Son of God,
who is and remains
true and eternal God,[1]
took to himself,
through the working of the Holy Spirit,[2]
from the flesh and blood of the virgin Mary,[3]
a truly human nature
so that he might also become David's true descendant,[4]
like his brothers and sisters in every way[5]
except for sin.[6]

[1] John 1:1; 10:30-36; Acts 13:33 (Ps. 2:7); Col. 1:15-17; 1 John 5:20
[2] Luke 1:35
[3] Matt. 1:18-23; John 1:14; Gal. 4:4; Heb. 2:14
[4] 2 Sam. 7:12-16; Ps. 132:11; Matt. 1:1; Rom. 1:3
[5] Phil. 2:7; Heb. 2:17
[6] Heb. 4:15; 7:26-27

36 Q. **How does the holy conception and birth of Christ**
benefit you?

A. He is our mediator[1]
and, in God's sight,
he covers with his innocence and perfect holiness
my sinfulness in which I was conceived.[2]

[1] 1 Tim. 2:5-6; Heb. 9:13-15
[2] Rom. 8:3-4; 2 Cor. 5:21; Gal. 4:4-5; 1 Pet. 1:18-19

**37 Q. What do you understand
by the word "suffered"?**

A. That during his whole life on earth,
but especially at the end,
Christ sustained
in body and soul
the wrath of God against the sin of the whole human race.[1]

This he did in order that,
by his suffering as the only atoning sacrifice,[2]
he might deliver us, body and soul,
from eternal condemnation,[3]
and gain for us
God's grace,
righteousness,
and eternal life.[4]

[1] Isa. 53; 1 Pet. 2:24; 3:18
[2] Rom. 3:25; Heb. 10:14; 1 John 2:2; 4:10
[3] Rom. 8:1-4; Gal. 3:13
[4] John 3:16; Rom. 3:24-26

**38 Q. Why did he suffer
"under Pontius Pilate" as judge?**

A. So that he,
though innocent,
might be condemned by an earthly judge,[1]
and so free us from the severe judgment of God
that was to fall on us.[2]

[1] Luke 23:13-24; John 19:4, 12-16
[2] Isa. 53:4-5; 2 Cor. 5:21; Gal. 3:13

**39 Q. Is it significant that he was "crucified"
instead of dying some other way?**

A. Yes.

By this I am convinced
that he shouldered the curse
which lay on me,
since death by crucifixion was cursed by God.[1]

[1] Gal. 3:10-13 (Deut. 21:23)

LORD'S DAY 16

40 Q. Why did Christ have to suffer death?

A. Because God's justice and truth require it: [1]
nothing else could pay for our sins
except the death of the Son of God.[2]

[1] Gen. 2:17
[2] Rom. 8:3-4; Phil. 2:8; Heb. 2:9

41 Q. Why was he "buried"?

A. His burial testifies
that he really died.[1]

[1] Isa. 53:9; John 19:38-42; Acts 13:29; 1 Cor. 15:3-4

**42 Q. Since Christ has died for us,
why do we still have to die?**

A. Our death does not pay the debt of our sins.[1]
Rather, it puts an end to our sinning
and is our entrance into eternal life.[2]

[1] Ps. 49:7
[2] John 5:24; Phil. 1:21-23; 1 Thess. 5:9-10

43 Q. **What further benefit do we receive**
from Christ's sacrifice and death on the cross?

A. By Christ's power
our old selves are crucified, put to death, and buried with him,[1]
so that the evil desires of the flesh
may no longer rule us,[2]
but that instead we may offer ourselves
as a sacrifice of gratitude to him.[3]

[1] Rom. 6:5-11; Col. 2:11-12
[2] Rom. 6:12-14
[3] Rom. 12:1; Eph. 5:1-2

44 Q. **Why does the creed add,**
"He descended to hell"?

A. To assure me during attacks of deepest dread and temptation
that Christ my Lord,
by suffering unspeakable anguish, pain, and terror of soul,
on the cross but also earlier,
has delivered me from hellish anguish and torment.[1]

[1] Isa. 53; Matt. 26:36-46; 27:45-46; Luke 22:44; Heb. 5:7-10

45 **Q. How does Christ's resurrection
benefit us?**

A. First, by his resurrection he has overcome death,
so that he might make us share in the righteousness
he obtained for us by his death.[1]

Second, by his power we too
are already raised to a new life.[2]

Third, Christ's resurrection
is a sure pledge to us of our blessed resurrection.[3]

[1] Rom. 4:25; 1 Cor. 15:16-20; 1 Pet. 1:3-5
[2] Rom. 6:5-11; Eph. 2:4-6; Col. 3:1-4
[3] Rom. 8:11; 1 Cor. 15:12-23; Phil. 3:20-21

LORD'S DAY 18

46 **Q. What do you mean by saying,
"He ascended to heaven"?**

A. That Christ,
while his disciples watched,
was taken up from the earth into heaven[1]
and remains there on our behalf[2]
until he comes again
to judge the living and the dead.[3]

[1] Luke 24:50-51; Acts 1:9-11
[2] Rom. 8:34; Eph. 4:8-10; Heb. 7:23-25; 9:24
[3] Acts 1:11

47 Q. But isn't Christ with us
until the end of the world
as he promised us?[1]

A. Christ is true human and true God.
In his human nature Christ is not now on earth;[2]
but in his divinity, majesty, grace, and Spirit
he is never absent from us.[3]

[1] Matt. 28:20
[2] Acts 1:9-11; 3:19-21
[3] Matt. 28:18-20; John 14:16-19

48 Q. If his humanity is not present
wherever his divinity is,
then aren't the two natures of Christ
separated from each other?

A. Certainly not.
Since divinity
is not limited
and is present everywhere,[1]
it is evident that
Christ's divinity is surely beyond the bounds of
the humanity that has been taken on,
but at the same time his divinity is in
and remains personally united to
his humanity.[2]

[1] Jer. 23:23-24; Acts 7:48-49 (Isa. 66:1)
[2] John 1:14; 3:13; Col. 2:9

**49 Q. How does Christ's ascension to heaven
benefit us?**

A. First, he is our advocate
in heaven
in the presence of his Father.[1]

Second, we have our own flesh in heaven
as a sure pledge that Christ our head
will also take us, his members,
up to himself.[2]

Third, he sends his Spirit to us on earth
as a corresponding pledge.[3]
By the Spirit's power
we seek not earthly things
but the things above, where Christ is,
sitting at God's right hand.[4]

[1] Rom. 8:34; 1 John 2:1
[2] John 14:2; 17:24; Eph. 2:4-6
[3] John 14:16; 2 Cor. 1:21-22; 5:5
[4] Col. 3:1-4

LORD'S DAY 19

**50 Q. Why the next words:
"and is seated at the right hand of God"?**

A. Because Christ ascended to heaven
to show there that he is head of his church,[1]
the one through whom the Father rules all things.[2]

[1] Eph. 1:20-23; Col. 1:18
[2] Matt. 28:18; John 5:22-23

51 Q. How does this glory of Christ our head benefit us?

A. First, through his Holy Spirit
    he pours out gifts from heaven
        upon us his members.[1]

Second, by his power
    he defends us and keeps us safe
        from all enemies.[2]

[1] Acts 2:33; Eph. 4:7-12
[2] Ps. 110:1-2; John 10:27-30; Rev. 19:11-16

52 Q. How does Christ's return "to judge the living and the dead" comfort you?

A. In all distress and persecution,
    with uplifted head,
    I confidently await the very judge
        who has already offered himself to the judgment of God
        in my place and removed the whole curse from me.[1]
Christ will cast all his enemies and mine
    into everlasting condemnation,
but will take me and all his chosen ones
    to himself
    into the joy and glory of heaven.[2]

[1] Luke 21:28; Rom. 8:22-25; Phil. 3:20-21; Tit. 2:13-14
[2] Matt. 25:31-46; 2 Thess. 1:6-10

LORD'S DAY 20

**53 Q. What do you believe
concerning "the Holy Spirit"?**

A. First, that the Spirit, with the Father and the Son,
is eternal God.[1]

Second, that the Spirit is given also to me,[2]
so that, through true faith,
he makes me share in Christ and all his benefits,[3]
comforts me,[4]
and will remain with me forever.[5]

[1] Gen. 1:1-2; Matt. 28:19; Acts 5:3-4
[2] 1 Cor. 6:19; 2 Cor. 1:21-22; Gal. 4:6
[3] Gal. 3:14
[4] John 15:26; Acts 9:31
[5] John 14:16-17; 1 Pet. 4:14

**54 Q. What do you believe
concerning "the holy catholic church"?**

A. I believe that the Son of God
through his Spirit and Word,[1]
out of the entire human race,[2]
from the beginning of the world to its end,[3]
gathers, protects, and preserves for himself
a community chosen for eternal life[4]
and united in true faith.[5]
And of this community I am[6] and always will be[7]
a living member.

[1] John 10:14-16; Acts 20:28; Rom. 10:14-17; Col. 1:18
[2] Gen. 26:3b-4; Rev. 5:9
[3] Isa. 59:21; 1 Cor. 11:26
[4] Matt. 16:18; John 10:28-30; Rom. 8:28-30; Eph. 1:3-14
[5] Acts 2:42-47; Eph. 4:1-6
[6] 1 John 3:14, 19-21
[7] John 10:27-28; 1 Cor. 1:4-9; 1 Pet. 1:3-5

**55 Q. What do you understand by
"the communion of saints"?**

A. First, that believers one and all,
as members of this community,
share in Christ
and in all his treasures and gifts.[1]
Second, that each member
should consider it a duty
to use these gifts
readily and joyfully
for the service and enrichment
of the other members.[2]

[1] Rom. 8:32; 1 Cor. 6:17; 12:4-7, 12-13; 1 John 1:3
[2] Rom. 12:4-8; 1 Cor. 12:20-27; 13:1-7; Phil. 2:4-8

56 Q. What do you believe
concerning "the forgiveness of sins"?

A. I believe that God,
because of Christ's satisfaction,
will no longer remember
any of my sins[1]
or my sinful nature
which I need to struggle against all my life.[2]

Rather, by grace
God grants me the righteousness of Christ
to free me forever from judgment.[3]

[1] Ps. 103:3-4, 10, 12; Mic. 7:18-19; 2 Cor. 5:18-21; 1 John 1:7; 2:2
[2] Rom. 7:21-25
[3] John 3:17-18; Rom. 8:1-2

LORD'S DAY 22

57 Q. How does "the resurrection of the body"
comfort you?

A. Not only will my soul
be taken immediately after this life
to Christ its head,[1]
but also my very flesh will be
raised by the power of Christ,
reunited with my soul,
and made like Christ's glorious body.[2]

[1] Luke 23:43; Phil. 1:21-23
[2] 1 Cor. 15:20, 42-46, 54; Phil. 3:21; 1 John 3:2

58 Q. How does the article concerning "life everlasting" comfort you?

A. Even as I already now
   experience in my heart
   the beginning of eternal joy,[1]
so after this life I will have
   perfect blessedness such as
      no eye has seen,
      no ear has heard,
      no human heart has ever imagined:
a blessedness in which to praise God forever.[2]

[1] Rom. 14:17
[2] John 17:3; 1 Cor. 2:9

LORD'S DAY 23

59 Q. What good does it do you, however, to believe all this?

A. In Christ I am righteous before God
   and heir to life everlasting.[1]

[1] John 3:36; Rom. 1:17 (Hab. 2:4); Rom. 5:1-2

60 Q. How are you righteous before God?

   A. Only by true faith in Jesus Christ.[1]

Even though my conscience accuses me
   of having grievously sinned against all God's
      commandments,
   of never having kept any of them,[2]
   and of still being inclined toward all evil,[3]
nevertheless,
   without any merit of my own,[4]
   out of sheer grace,[5]
God grants and credits to me
the perfect satisfaction, righteousness, and holiness of Christ,[6]
   as if I had never sinned nor been a sinner,
   and as if I had been as perfectly obedient
      as Christ was obedient for me.[7]

All I need to do
is accept this gift with a believing heart.[8]

[1] Rom. 3:21-28; Gal. 2:16; Eph. 2:8-9; Phil 3:8-11
[2] Rom. 3:9-10
[3] Rom. 7:23
[4] Tit. 3:4-5
[5] Rom. 3:24; Eph. 2:8
[6] Rom. 4:3-5 (Gen. 15:6); 2 Cor. 5:17-19; 1 John 2:1-2
[7] Rom. 4:24-25; 2 Cor. 5:21
[8] John 3:18; Acts 16:30-31

**61 Q. Why do you say that
through faith alone
you are righteous?**

A. Not because I please God
by the worthiness of my faith.
It is because only Christ's satisfaction, righteousness, and
holiness
make me righteous before God,[1]
and because I can accept this righteousness and make it mine
in no other way
than through faith.[2]

[1] 1 Cor. 1:30-31
[2] Rom. 10:10; 1 John 5:10-12

LORD'S DAY 24

**62 Q. Why can't our good works
be our righteousness before God,
or at least a part of our righteousness?**

A. Because the righteousness
which can pass God's judgment
must be entirely perfect
and must in every way measure up to the divine law.[1]
But even our best works in this life
are imperfect
and stained with sin.[2]

[1] Rom. 3:20; Gal. 3:10 (Deut. 27:26)
[2] Isa. 64:6

63 Q. **How can our good works**
    be said to merit nothing
    when God promises to reward them
    in this life and the next?[1]

A. This reward is not earned;
    it is a gift of grace.[2]

[1] Matt. 5:12; Heb. 11:6
[2] Luke 17:10; 2 Tim. 4:7-8

64 Q. **But doesn't this teaching**
    make people indifferent and wicked?

A. No.
    It is impossible
        for those grafted into Christ through true faith
    not to produce fruits of gratitude.[1]

[1] Luke 6:43-45; John 15:5

The Holy Sacraments

LORD'S DAY 25

65 Q. **It is through faith alone**
    that we share in Christ and all his benefits:
    where then does that faith come from?

A. The Holy Spirit produces it in our hearts[1]
        by the preaching of the holy gospel,[2]
    and confirms it
        by the use of the holy sacraments.[3]

[1] John 3:5; 1 Cor. 2:10-14; Eph. 2:8
[2] Rom. 10:17; 1 Pet. 1:23-25
[3] Matt. 28:19-20; 1 Cor. 10:16

66 Q. What are sacraments?

A. Sacraments are visible, holy signs and seals.
They were instituted by God so that
by our use of them
he might make us understand more clearly
the promise of the gospel,
and seal that promise.[1]

And this is God's gospel promise:
to grant us forgiveness of sins and eternal life
by grace
because of Christ's one sacrifice
accomplished on the cross.[2]

[1] Gen. 17:11; Deut. 30:6; Rom. 4:11
[2] Matt. 26:27-28; Acts 2:38; Heb. 10:10

**67 Q. Are both the word and the sacraments then
intended to focus our faith
on the sacrifice of Jesus Christ on the cross
as the only ground of our salvation?**

A. Yes!
In the gospel the Holy Spirit teaches us
and by the holy sacraments confirms
that our entire salvation
rests on Christ's one sacrifice for us on the cross.[1]

[1] Rom. 6:3; 1 Cor. 11:26; Gal. 3:27

**68 Q. How many sacraments
did Christ institute in the New Testament?**

A. Two: holy baptism and the holy supper.[1]

[1] Matt. 28:19-20; 1 Cor. 11:23-26

Holy Baptism

LORD'S DAY 26

**69 Q. How does holy baptism
remind and assure you
that Christ's one sacrifice on the cross
benefits you personally?**

A. In this way:
Christ instituted this outward washing[1]
and with it promised that,
as surely as water washes away the dirt from the body,
so certainly his blood and his Spirit
wash away my soul's impurity,
that is, all my sins.[2]

[1] Acts 2:38
[2] Matt. 3:11; Rom. 6:3-10; 1 Pet. 3:21

70 Q. **What does it mean**
to be washed with Christ's blood and Spirit?

A. To be washed with Christ's blood means
that God, by grace, has forgiven our sins
because of Christ's blood
poured out for us in his sacrifice on the cross.[1]

To be washed with Christ's Spirit means
that the Holy Spirit has renewed
and sanctified us to be members of Christ,
so that more and more
we become dead to sin
and live holy and blameless lives.[2]

[1] Zech. 13:1; Eph. 1:7-8; Heb. 12:24; 1 Pet. 1:2; Rev. 1:5
[2] Ezek. 36:25-27; John 3:5-8; Rom. 6:4; 1 Cor. 6:11; Col. 2:11-12

71 Q. **Where does Christ promise**
that we are washed with his blood and Spirit
as surely as we are washed
with the water of baptism?

A. In the institution of baptism, where he says:

"Go therefore and make disciples of all nations,
baptizing them in the name of the Father
and of the Son
and of the Holy Spirit."[1]

"The one who believes and is baptized will be saved;
but the one who does not believe will be condemned."[2]

This promise is repeated when Scripture calls baptism
"the water of rebirth"[3] and
the washing away of sins.[4]

[1] Matt. 28:19
[2] Mark 16:16
[3] Tit. 3:5
[4] Acts 22:16

LORD'S DAY 27

72 Q. **Does this outward washing with water**
itself wash away sins?

A. No, only Jesus Christ's blood and the Holy Spirit
cleanse us from all sins.[1]

[1] Matt. 3:11; 1 Pet. 3:21; 1 John 1:7

73 Q. **Why then does the Holy Spirit call baptism**
    the water of rebirth and
    the washing away of sins?

A. God has good reason for these words.
    To begin with, God wants to teach us that
        the blood and Spirit of Christ take away our sins
        just as water removes dirt from the body.[1]

    But more important,
    God wants to assure us, by this divine pledge and sign,
        that we are as truly washed of our sins spiritually
        as our bodies are washed with water physically.[2]

[1] 1 Cor. 6:11; Rev. 1:5; 7:14
[2] Acts 2:38; Rom. 6:3-4; Gal. 3:27

73 Q. **Should infants also be baptized?**

A. Yes.
    Infants as well as adults
        are included in God's covenant and people,[1]
    and they, no less than adults, are promised
        deliverance from sin through Christ's blood
        and the Holy Spirit who produces faith.[2]

    Therefore, by baptism, the sign of the covenant,
        they too should be incorporated into the Christian church
        and distinguished from the children
            of unbelievers.[3]
    This was done in the Old Testament by circumcision,[4]
        which was replaced in the New Testament by baptism.[5]

[1] Gen. 17:7; Matt. 19:14
[2] Isa. 44:1-3; Acts 2:38-39; 16:31
[3] Acts 10:47; 1 Cor. 7:14
[4] Gen. 17:9-14
[5] Col. 2:11-13

LORD'S DAY 28

75 **Q. How does the holy supper
remind and assure you
that you share in
Christ's one sacrifice on the cross
and in all his benefits?**

   A. In this way:
Christ has commanded me and all believers
to eat this broken bread and to drink this cup
in remembrance of him.
With this command come these promises:[1]

First,
    as surely as I see with my eyes
        the bread of the Lord broken for me
        and the cup shared with me,
    so surely
        his body was offered and broken for me
        and his blood poured out for me
            on the cross.

Second,
    as surely as
        I receive from the hand of the one who serves,
        and taste with my mouth
            the bread and cup of the Lord,
            given me as sure signs of Christ's body and blood,
    so surely
        he nourishes and refreshes my soul for eternal life
        with his crucified body and poured-out blood.

[1] Matt. 26:26-28; Mark 14:22-24; Luke 22:19-20; 1 Cor. 11:23-25

76   Q.   **What does it mean**
to eat the crucified body of Christ
and to drink his poured-out blood?

A.   It means
to accept with a believing heart
the entire suffering and death of Christ
and thereby
to receive forgiveness of sins and eternal life.[1]

But it means more.
Through the Holy Spirit, who lives both in Christ and in us,
we are united more and more to Christ's blessed body.[2]
And so, although he is in heaven[3] and we are on earth,
we are flesh of his flesh and bone of his bone.[4]
And we forever live on and are governed by one Spirit,
as the members of our body are by one soul.[5]

[1] John 6:35, 40, 50-54
[2] John 6:55-56; 1 Cor. 12:13
[3] Acts 1:9-11; 1 Cor. 11:26; Col. 3:1
[4] 1 Cor. 6:15-17; Eph. 5:29-30; 1 John 4:13
[5] John 6:56-58; 15:1-6; Eph. 4:15-16; 1 John 3:24

**77 Q. Where does Christ promise
to nourish and refresh believers
with his body and blood
as surely as
they eat this broken bread
and drink this cup?**

A. In the institution of the Lord's Supper:

> "The Lord Jesus on the night when he was betrayed
> took a loaf of bread, and when he had given thanks,
> he broke it and said,
>> 'This is my body that is [broken]* for you.
>> Do this in remembrance of me.'
> In the same way he took the cup also, after supper, saying,
>> 'This cup is the new covenant in my blood.
>> Do this, as often as you drink it,
>> in remembrance of me.'
> For as often as you eat this bread and drink the cup,
> you proclaim the Lord's death
> until he comes."[1]

This promise is repeated by Paul in these words:

> "The cup of blessing that we bless,
>> is it not a sharing in the blood of Christ?
> The bread that we break,
>> is it not a sharing in the body of Christ?
> Because there is one bread, we who are many are one body,
> for we all partake of the one bread."[2]

---

[1] 1 Cor. 11:23-26
[2] 1 Cor. 10:16-17
*The word "broken" does not appear in the NRSV text, but it was present in the original German of the Heidelberg Catechism.

**78 Q. Do the bread and wine become
the real body and blood of Christ?**

A. No.
Just as the water of baptism
is not changed into Christ's blood
and does not itself wash away sins
but is simply a divine sign and assurance[1] of these things,
so too the holy bread of the Lord's Supper
does not become the actual body of Christ,[2]
even though it is called the body of Christ[3]
in keeping with the nature and language of sacraments.[4]

[1] Eph. 5:26; Tit. 3:5
[2] Matt. 26:26-29
[3] 1 Cor. 10:16-17; 11:26-28
[4] Gen. 17:10-11; Ex. 12:11, 13; 1 Cor. 10:1-4

79 Q. **Why then does Christ call**
the bread his body
and the cup his blood,
    or the new covenant in his blood,
and Paul use the words,
a sharing in Christ's body and blood?

A. Christ has good reason for these words.
He wants to teach us that
    just as bread and wine nourish the temporal life,
    so too his crucified body and poured-out blood
    are the true food and drink of our souls for eternal life.[1]

But more important,
he wants to assure us, by this visible sign and pledge,
    that we, through the Holy Spirit's work,
        share in his true body and blood
        as surely as our mouths
        receive these holy signs in his remembrance,[2]
    and that all of his suffering and obedience
        are as definitely ours
        as if we personally
        had suffered and made satisfaction for our sins.[3]

[1] John 6:51, 55
[2] 1 Cor. 10:16-17; 11:26
[3] Rom. 6:5-11

LORD'S DAY 30

80* Q. **How does the Lord's Supper**
differ from the Roman Catholic Mass?

A. The Lord's Supper declares to us
    that all our sins are completely forgiven
    through the one sacrifice of Jesus Christ,
    which he himself accomplished on the cross once for all.[1]

It also declares to us
that the Holy Spirit grafts us into Christ,[2]
who with his true body
is now in heaven at the right hand of the Father[3]
where he wants us to worship him.[4]

[But the Mass teaches
that the living and the dead
do not have their sins forgiven
through the suffering of Christ
unless Christ is still offered for them daily by the priests.
It also teaches
that Christ is bodily present
under the form of bread and wine
where Christ is therefore to be worshiped.
Thus the Mass is basically
nothing but a denial
of the one sacrifice and suffering of Jesus Christ
and a condemnable idolatry.]**

[1] John 19:30; Heb. 7:27; 9:12, 25-26; 10:10-18
[2] 1 Cor. 6:17; 10:16-17
[3] Acts 7:55-56; Heb. 1:3; 8:1
[4] Matt. 6:20-21; John 4:21-24; Phil. 3:20; Col. 3:1-3

*Q&A 80 was altogether absent from the first edition of the catechism but was present in a shorter form in the second edition. The translation here given is of the expanded text of the third edition.

**In response to a mandate from Synod 1998, the Christian Reformed Church's Inter-church Relations Committee conducted a study of Q&A 80 and the Roman Catholic Mass. Based on this study, Synod 2004 declared that "Q&A 80 can no longer be held in its current form as part of our confession." Synod 2006 directed that Q&A 80 remain in the CRC's text of the Heidelberg Catechism but that the last three paragraphs be placed in brackets to indicate that they do not accurately reflect the official teaching and practice of today's Roman Catholic Church and are no longer confessionally binding on members of the CRC.

The Reformed Church in America and the Presbyterian Church (USA) retain the original full text, choosing to recognize that the catechism was written within a historical context which may not accurately describe the Roman Catholic Church's current stance.

81 Q. **Who should come
to the Lord's table?**

A. Those who are displeased with themselves
because of their sins,
but who nevertheless trust
that their sins are pardoned
and that their remaining weakness is covered
by the suffering and death of Christ,
and who also desire more and more
to strengthen their faith
and to lead a better life.

Hypocrites and those who are unrepentant, however,
eat and drink judgment on themselves.[1]

[1] 1 Cor. 10:19-22; 11:26-32

82 Q. **Should those be admitted
to the Lord's Supper
who show by what they profess and how they live
that they are unbelieving and ungodly?**

A. No, that would dishonor God's covenant
and bring down God's wrath upon the entire congregation.[1]
Therefore, according to the instruction of Christ
and his apostles,
the Christian church is duty-bound to exclude such people,
by the official use of the keys of the kingdom,
until they reform their lives.

[1] 1 Cor. 11:17-32; Ps. 50:14-16; Isa. 1:11-17

83 Q. What are the keys of the kingdom?

A. The preaching of the holy gospel
and Christian discipline toward repentance.
Both of them
    open the kingdom of heaven to believers
    and close it to unbelievers.[1]

[1] Matt. 16:19; John 20:22-23

**84 Q. How does preaching the holy gospel
open and close the kingdom of heaven?**

A. According to the command of Christ:

The kingdom of heaven is opened
by proclaiming and publicly declaring
    to all believers, each and every one, that,
    as often as they accept the gospel promise in true faith,
    God, because of Christ's merit,
    truly forgives all their sins.

The kingdom of heaven is closed, however,
by proclaiming and publicly declaring
    to unbelievers and hypocrites that,
    as long as they do not repent,
    the wrath of God and eternal condemnation
    rest on them.

God's judgment, both in this life and in the life to come,
is based on this gospel testimony.[1]

[1] Matt. 16:19; John 3:31-36; 20:21-23

**85 Q. How is the kingdom of heaven
closed and opened by Christian discipline?**

A. According to the command of Christ:

Those who, though called Christians,
profess unchristian teachings or live unchristian lives,
and who after repeated personal and loving admonitions,
refuse to abandon their errors and evil ways,
and who after being reported to the church, that is,
to those ordained by the church for that purpose,
fail to respond also to the church's admonitions—
such persons the church excludes
from the Christian community
by withholding the sacraments from them,
and God also excludes them from the kingdom of Christ.[1]

Such persons,
when promising and demonstrating genuine reform,
are received again
as members of Christ
and of his church.[2]

---

[1] Matt. 18:15-20; 1 Cor. 5:3-5, 11-13; 2 Thess. 3:14-15
[2] Luke 15:20-24; 2 Cor. 2:6-11

Part III: Gratitude

LORD'S DAY 32

86 Q. **Since we have been delivered**
from our misery
by grace through Christ
without any merit of our own,
why then should we do good works?

A. Because Christ, having redeemed us by his blood,
is also restoring us by his Spirit into his image,
so that with our whole lives
we may show that we are thankful to God
for his benefits,[1]
so that he may be praised through us,[2]
so that we may be assured of our faith by its fruits,[3]
and so that by our godly living
our neighbors may be won over to Christ.[4]

[1] Rom. 6:13; 12:1-2; 1 Pet. 2:5-10
[2] Matt. 5:16; 1 Cor. 6:19-20
[3] Matt. 7:17-18; Gal. 5:22-24; 2 Pet. 1:10-11
[4] Matt. 5:14-16; Rom. 14:17-19; 1 Pet. 2:12; 3:1-2

87 Q. Can those be saved
who do not turn to God
from their ungrateful
and unrepentant ways?

A. By no means.
Scripture tells us that
no unchaste person,
no idolater, adulterer, thief,
no covetous person,
no drunkard, slanderer, robber,
or the like
will inherit the kingdom of God.[1]

[1] 1 Cor. 6:9-10; Gal. 5:19-21; Eph. 5:1-20; 1 John 3:14

LORD'S DAY 33

88 Q. What is involved
in genuine repentance or conversion?

A. Two things:
the dying-away of the old self,
and the rising-to-life of the new.[1]

[1] Rom. 6:1-11; 2 Cor. 5:17; Eph. 4:22-24; Col. 3:5-10

89 Q. What is the dying-away of the old self?

A. To be genuinely sorry for sin
and more and more to hate
and run away from it.[1]

[1] Ps. 51:3-4, 17; Joel 2:12-13; Rom. 8:12-13; 2 Cor. 7:10

90 Q. What is the rising-to-life of the new self?

   A. Wholehearted joy in God through Christ[1]
      and a love and delight to live
         according to the will of God
         by doing every kind of good work.[2]

[1] Ps. 51:8, 12; Isa.57:15; Rom. 5:1; 14:17
[2] Rom. 6:10-11; Gal. 2:20

91 Q. What are good works?

   A. Only those which
         are done out of true faith,[1]
         conform to God's law,[2]
         and are done for God's glory;[3]
      and not those based
         on our own opinion
         or human tradition.[4]

[1] John 15:5; Heb. 11:6
[2] Lev. 18:4; 1 Sam. 15:22; Eph. 2:10
[3] 1 Cor. 10:31
[4] Deut. 12:32; Isa. 29:13; Ezek. 20:18-19; Matt. 15:7-9

LORD'S DAY 34

92 Q. What is God's law?

A. God spoke all these words:

THE FIRST COMMANDMENT

"I am the LORD your God,
 who brought you out of the land of Egypt,
 out of the house of slavery;
you shall have no other gods before me."

THE SECOND COMMANDMENT

"You shall not make for yourself an idol,
 whether in the form of anything that is in heaven above,
 or that is on the earth beneath,
 or that is in the water under the earth.
You shall not bow down to them or worship them;
 for I the LORD your God am a jealous God,
 punishing children for the iniquity of parents,
  to the third and the fourth generation
  of those who reject me,
 but showing love to the thousandth generation of those
  who love me and keep my commandments."

THE THIRD COMMANDMENT

"You shall not make wrongful use of the name of the LORD
  your God,
 for the LORD will not acquit anyone
 who misuses his name."

THE FOURTH COMMANDMENT

"Remember the sabbath day, and keep it holy.
Six days you shall labor and do all your work.
But the seventh day is a sabbath to the LORD your God;
you shall not do any work—
    you, your son or your daughter,
    your male or female slave,
    your livestock,
    or the alien resident in your towns.
For in six days the LORD made
    heaven and earth, the sea,
    and all that is in them,
but rested the seventh day;
therefore the LORD blessed the sabbath day
and consecrated it."

THE FIFTH COMMANDMENT

"Honor your father and your mother,
    so that your days may be long
    in the land that the LORD your God is giving to you."

THE SIXTH COMMANDMENT

"You shall not murder."

THE SEVENTH COMMANDMENT

"You shall not commit adultery."

THE EIGHTH COMMANDMENT

"You shall not steal."

THE NINTH COMMANDMENT

"You shall not bear false witness
    against your neighbor."

THE TENTH COMMANDMENT

"You shall not covet your neighbor's house;
you shall not covet your neighbor's wife,
 or male or female slave,
 or ox, or donkey,
 or anything that belongs to your neighbor."[1]

[1] Ex. 20:1-17; Deut. 5:6-21

93 Q. How are these commandments divided?
  A. Into two tables.
    The first has four commandments,
      teaching us how we ought to live in relation to God.
    The second has six commandments,
      teaching us what we owe our neighbor.[1]

[1] Matt. 22:37-39

**94 Q. What does the Lord require
in the first commandment?**

A. That I, not wanting to endanger my own salvation,
avoid and shun

all idolatry,[1] sorcery, superstitious rites,[2]
and prayer to saints or to other creatures.[3]

That I rightly know the only true God,[4]
trust him alone,[5]
and look to God for every good thing[6]
humbly[7] and patiently,[8]
and love,[9] fear,[10] and honor[11] God
with all my heart.

In short,
that I give up anything
rather than go against God's will in any way.[12]

[1] 1 Cor. 6:9-10; 10:5-14; 1 John 5:21
[2] Lev. 19:31; Deut. 18:9-12
[3] Matt. 4:10; Rev. 19:10; 22:8-9
[4] John 17:3
[5] Jer. 17:5, 7
[6] Ps. 104:27-28; James 1:17
[7] 1 Pet. 5:5-6
[8] Col. 1:11; Heb. 10:36
[9] Matt. 22:37 (Deut. 6:5)
[10] Prov. 9:10; 1 Pet. 1:17
[11] Matt. 4:10 (Deut. 6:13)
[12] Matt. 5:29-30; 10:37-39

95 Q. What is idolatry?

A. Idolatry is

having or inventing something in which one trusts
in place of or alongside of the only true God,
who has revealed himself in the Word.[1]

[1] 1 Chron. 16:26; Gal. 4:8-9; Eph. 5:5; Phil. 3:19

**96 Q. What is God's will for us
in the second commandment?**

A. That we in no way make any image of God[1]
nor worship him in any other way
than has been commanded in God's Word.[2]

[1] Deut. 4:15-19; Isa. 40:18-25; Acts 17:29; Rom. 1:22-23
[2] Lev. 10:1-7; 1 Sam. 15:22-23; John 4:23-24

**97 Q. May we then not make
any image at all?**

A. God can not and may not
be visibly portrayed in any way.

Although creatures may be portrayed,
yet God forbids making or having such images
if one's intention is to worship them
or to serve God through them.[1]

[1] Ex. 34:13-14, 17; 2 Kings 18:4-5

**98 Q. But may not images be permitted in churches
in place of books for the unlearned?**

A. No, we should not try to be wiser than God.
God wants the Christian community instructed
by the living preaching of his Word—[1]
not by idols that cannot even talk.[2]

[1] Rom. 10:14-15, 17; 2 Tim. 3:16-17; 2 Pet. 1:19
[2] Jer. 10:8; Hab. 2:18-20

99 Q. What is the aim of the third commandment?

A. That we neither blaspheme nor misuse the name of God
   by cursing,[1] perjury,[2] or unnecessary oaths,[3]
nor share in such horrible sins
   by being silent bystanders.[4]

In summary,
   we should use the holy name of God
      only with reverence and awe,[5]
   so that we may properly
      confess God,[6]
      pray to God,[7]
      and glorify God in all our words and works.[8]

[1] Lev. 24:10-17
[2] Lev. 19:12
[3] Matt. 5:37; James 5:12
[4] Lev. 5:1; Prov. 29:24
[5] Ps. 99:1-5; Jer. 4:2
[6] Matt. 10:32-33; Rom. 10:9-10
[7] Ps. 50:14-15; 1 Tim. 2:8
[8] Col. 3:17

100 Q. Is blasphemy of God's name by swearing and cursing
really such serious sin
that God is angry also with those
who do not do all they can
to help prevent and forbid it?

A. Yes, indeed.[1]
No sin is greater
or provokes God's wrath more
than blaspheming his name.
That is why God commanded it to be punished with death.[2]

[1] Lev. 5:1
[2] Lev. 24:10-17

LORD'S DAY 37

101 Q. But may we swear an oath in God's name
if we do it reverently?

A. Yes, when the government demands it,
or when necessity requires it,
in order to maintain and promote truth and trustworthiness
for God's glory and our neighbor's good.
Such oaths are grounded in God's Word[1]
and were rightly used by the people of God
in the Old and New Testaments.[2]

[1] Deut. 6:13; 10:20; Jer. 4:1-2; Heb. 6:16
[2] Gen. 21:24; Josh. 9:15; 1 Kings 1:29-30; Rom. 1:9; 2 Cor. 1:23

102 Q. May we also swear by saints or other creatures?

A. No.

A legitimate oath means calling upon God
as the only one who knows my heart
to witness to my truthfulness
and to punish me if I swear falsely.[1]
No creature is worthy of such honor.[2]

[1] Rom. 9:1; 2 Cor. 1:23
[2] Matt. 5:34-37; 23:16-22; James 5:12

LORD'S DAY 38

**103 Q. What is God's will for you
in the fourth commandment?**

A. First,

that the gospel ministry and education for it be maintained,[1]
and that, especially on the festive day of rest,
I diligently attend the assembly of God's people[2]
to learn what God's Word teaches,[3]
to participate in the sacraments,[4]
to pray to God publicly,[5]
and to bring Christian offerings for the poor.[6]

Second,

that every day of my life
I rest from my evil ways,
let the Lord work in me through his Spirit,
and so begin in this life
the eternal Sabbath.[7]

[1] Deut. 6:4-9, 20-25; 1 Cor. 9:13-14; 2 Tim. 2:2; 3:13-17; Tit. 1:5
[2] Deut. 12:5-12; Ps. 40:9-10; 68:26; Acts 2:42-47; Heb. 10:23-25
[3] Rom. 10:14-17; 1 Cor. 14:31-32; 1 Tim. 4:13
[4] 1 Cor. 11:23-25
[5] Col. 3:16; 1 Tim. 2:1
[6] Ps. 50:14; 1 Cor. 16:2; 2 Cor. 8 & 9
[7] Isa. 66:23; Heb. 4:9-11

LORD'S DAY 39

104 Q. **What is God's will for you
in the fifth commandment?**

A. That I honor, love, and be loyal
to my father and mother
and all those in authority over me;
that I submit myself with proper obedience
to all their good teaching and discipline;[1]
and also that I be patient with their failings—[2]
for through them God chooses to rule us.[3]

[1] Ex. 21:17; Prov. 1:8; 4:1; Rom. 13:1-2; Eph. 5:21-22; 6:1-9; Col. 3:18- 4:1
[2] Prov. 20:20; 23:22; 1 Pet. 2:18
[3] Matt. 22:21; Rom. 13:1-8; Eph. 6:1-9; Col. 3:18-21

LORD'S DAY 40

105 Q. **What is God's will for you
in the sixth commandment?**

A. I am not to belittle, hate, insult, or kill my neighbor—
not by my thoughts, my words, my look or gesture,
and certainly not by actual deeds—
and I am not to be party to this in others;[1]
rather, I am to put away all desire for revenge.[2]

I am not to harm or recklessly endanger myself either.[3]
Prevention of murder is also why
government is armed with the sword.[4]

[1] Gen. 9:6; Lev. 19:17-18; Matt. 5:21-22; 26:52
[2] Prov. 25:21-22; Matt. 18:35; Rom. 12:19; Eph. 4:26
[3] Matt. 4:7; 26:52; Rom. 13:11-14
[4] Gen. 9:6; Ex. 21:14; Rom. 13:4

106 Q. Does this commandment refer only to murder?

A. By forbidding murder God teaches us
that he hates the root of murder:
envy, hatred, anger, vindictiveness.[1]

In God's sight all such are disguised forms of murder.[2]

[1] Prov. 14:30; Rom. 1:29; 12:19; Gal. 5:19-21; 1 John 2:9-11
[2] 1 John 3:15

**107 Q. Is it enough then
that we do not murder our neighbor
in any such way?**

A. No.
By condemning envy, hatred, and anger
God wants us
to love our neighbors as ourselves,[1]
to be patient, peace-loving, gentle,
merciful, and friendly toward them,[2]
to protect them from harm as much as we can,
and to do good even to our enemies.[3]

[1] Matt. 7:12; 22:39; Rom. 12:10
[2] Matt. 5:3-12; Luke 6:36; Rom. 12:10, 18; Gal. 6:1-2; Eph. 4:2; Col. 3:12; 1 Pet. 3:8
[3] Ex. 23:4-5; Matt. 5:44-45; Rom. 12:20-21 (Prov. 25:21-22)

108 Q. What does the seventh commandment teach us?

  A. That God condemns all unchastity,[1]
  and that therefore we should thoroughly detest it[2]
  and live decent and chaste lives,[3]
  within or outside of the holy state of marriage.

[1] Lev. 18:30; Eph. 5:3-5
[2] Jude 22-23
[3] 1 Cor. 7:1-9; 1 Thess. 4:3-8; Heb. 13:4

**109 Q. Does God, in this commandment,
  forbid only such scandalous sins as adultery?**

  A. We are temples of the Holy Spirit, body and soul,
  and God wants both to be kept clean and holy.
  That is why God forbids
    all unchaste actions, looks, talk, thoughts, or desires,[1]
    and whatever may incite someone to them.[2]

[1] Matt. 5:27-29; 1 Cor. 6:18-20; Eph. 5:3-4
[2] 1 Cor. 15:33; Eph. 5:18

LORD'S DAY 42

110 Q. **What does God forbid**
in the eighth commandment?

    A. God forbids not only outright theft and robbery,
        punishable by law.[1]

    But in God's sight theft also includes
    all scheming and swindling
    in order to get our neighbor's goods for ourselves,
        whether by force or means that appear legitimate,[2]
        such as
            inaccurate measurements of weight, size, or volume;
            fraudulent merchandising;
            counterfeit money;
            excessive interest;
            or any other means forbidden by God.[3]

    In addition God forbids all greed[4]
    and pointless squandering of his gifts.[5]

[1] Ex. 22:1; 1 Cor. 5:9-10; 6:9-10
[2] Mic. 6:9-11; Luke 3:14; James 5:1-6
[3] Deut. 25:13-16; Ps. 15:5; Prov. 11:1; 12:22; Ezek. 45:9-12; Luke 6:35
[4] Luke 12:15; Eph. 5:5
[5] Prov. 21:20; 23:20-21; Luke 16:10-13

111 Q. **What does God require of you**
in this commandment?

   A. That I do whatever I can
      for my neighbor's good,
   that I treat others
      as I would like them to treat me,
   and that I work faithfully
      so that I may share with those in need.[1]

[1] Isa. 58:5-10; Matt. 7:12; Gal. 6:9-10; Eph. 4:28

LORD'S DAY 43

112 Q. **What is the aim of the ninth commandment?**

   A. That I
      never give false testimony against anyone,
      twist no one's words,
      not gossip or slander,
      nor join in condemning anyone
      rashly or without a hearing.[1]
   Rather, in court and everywhere else,
   I should avoid lying and deceit of every kind;
      these are the very devices the devil uses,
      and they would call down on me God's intense wrath.[2]
   I should love the truth,
      speak it candidly,
      and openly acknowledge it.[3]
   And I should do what I can
      to guard and advance my neighbor's good name.[4]

[1] Ps. 15; Prov. 19:5; Matt. 7:1; Luke 6:37; Rom. 1:28-32
[2] Lev. 19:11-12; Prov. 12:22; 13:5; John 8:44; Rev. 21:8
[3] 1 Cor. 13:6; Eph. 4:25
[4] 1 Pet. 3:8-9; 4:8

LORD'S DAY 44

113 Q.   What is the aim of the tenth commandment?

   A.   That not even the slightest desire or thought
          contrary to any one of God's commandments
          should ever arise in our hearts.

       Rather, with all our hearts
          we should always hate sin
          and take pleasure in whatever is right.[1]

[1] Ps. 19:7-14; 139:23-24; Rom. 7:7-8

**114 Q.   But can those converted to God
         obey these commandments perfectly?**

   A.   No.
       In this life even the holiest
       have only a small beginning of this obedience.[1]

       Nevertheless, with all seriousness of purpose,
       they do begin to live
       according to all, not only some,
       of God's commandments.[2]

[1] Eccles. 7:20; Rom. 7:14-15; 1 Cor. 13:9; 1 John 1:8-10
[2] Ps. 1:1-2; Rom. 7:22-25; Phil. 3:12-16

115 Q. **Since no one in this life**
can obey the Ten Commandments perfectly,
why does God want them
preached so pointedly?

 A. First, so that the longer we live
the more we may come to know our sinfulness
and the more eagerly look to Christ
for forgiveness of sins and righteousness.[1]

Second, so that
we may never stop striving,
and never stop praying to God for the grace of the Holy Spirit,
to be renewed more and more after God's image,
until after this life we reach our goal:
perfection.[2]

[1] Ps. 32:5; Rom. 3:19-26; 7:7, 24-25; 1 John 1:9
[2] 1 Cor. 9:24; Phil. 3:12-14; 1 John 3:1-3

The Lord's Prayer

LORD'S DAY 45

116 Q. **Why do Christians need to pray?**

 A. Because prayer is the most important part
of the thankfulness God requires of us.[1]
And also because God gives his grace and Holy Spirit
only to those who pray continually and groan inwardly,
asking God for these gifts
and thanking God for them.[2]

[1] Ps. 50:14-15; 116:12-19; 1 Thess. 5:16-18
[2] Matt. 7:7-8; Luke 11:9-13

117 Q. **What is the kind of prayer**
that pleases God and that he listens to?

A. First, we must pray from the heart
to no other than the one true God,
revealed to us in his Word,
asking for everything God has commanded us to ask for.[1]

Second, we must fully recognize our need and misery,
so that we humble ourselves in God's majestic presence.[2]
Third, we must rest on this unshakable foundation:
even though we do not deserve it,
God will surely listen to our prayer
because of Christ our Lord.
That is what God promised us in his Word.[3]

[1] Ps. 145:18-20; John 4:22-24; Rom. 8:26-27; James 1:5; 1 John 5:14-15
[2] 2 Chron. 7:14; Ps. 2:11; 34:18; 62:8; Isa. 66:2; Rev. 4
[3] Dan. 9:17-19; Matt. 7:8; John 14:13-14; 16:23; Rom. 10:13; James 1:6

118 Q. **What did God command us to pray for?**

A. Everything we need, spiritually and physically,[1]
as embraced in the prayer
Christ our Lord himself taught us.

[1] James 1:17; Matt. 6:33

119 Q. What is this prayer?

A. Our Father in heaven,
hallowed be your name.
Your kingdom come.
Your will be done,
on earth as it is in heaven.
Give us this day our daily bread.
And forgive us our debts,
as we also have forgiven our debtors.
And do not bring us to the time of trial,
but rescue us from the evil one.*
For the kingdom
and the power
and the glory are yours forever.
Amen.[1]**

[1] Matt. 6:9-13; Luke 11:2-4

*This text of the Lord's Prayer is from the New Revised Standard Version in keeping with the use of the NRSV throughout this edition of the catechism. Most biblical scholars agree that it is an accurate translation of the Greek text and carries virtually the same meaning as the more traditional text of the Lord's Prayer.

**Earlier and better manuscripts of Matthew 6 omit the words "For the kingdom and . . . Amen."

LORD'S DAY 46

**120 Q. Why did Christ command us
to call God "our Father"?**

    A. To awaken in us
       at the very beginning of our prayer
       what should be basic to our prayer—
          a childlike reverence and trust
          that through Christ God has become our Father,
       and that just as our parents do not refuse us
          the things of this life,
       even less will God our Father refuse to give us
          what we ask in faith.[1]

[1] Matt. 7:9-11; Luke 11:11-13

**121 Q. Why the words
"in heaven"?**

    A. These words teach us
         not to think of God's heavenly majesty
            as something earthly,[1]
         and to expect everything
            needed for body and soul
            from God's almighty power.[2]

[1] Jer. 23:23-24; Acts 17:24-25
[2] Matt. 6:25-34; Rom. 8:31-32

122 Q.   What does the first petition mean?

  A.   "Hallowed be your name" means:

> Help us to truly know you,[1]
> to honor, glorify, and praise you
>   for all your works
>   and for all that shines forth from them:
>   your almighty power, wisdom, kindness,
>   justice, mercy, and truth.[2]

> And it means,

> Help us to direct all our living—
>   what we think, say, and do—
> so that your name will never be blasphemed because of us
> but always honored and praised.[3]

[1] Jer. 9:23-24; 31:33-34; Matt. 16:17; John 17:3
[2] Ex. 34:5-8; Ps. 145; Jer. 32:16-20; Luke 1:46-55, 68-75; Rom. 11:33-36
[3] Ps. 115:1; Matt. 5:16

123 Q. What does the second petition mean?

A. "Your kingdom come" means:
Rule us by your Word and Spirit in such a way
    that more and more we submit to you.[1]

Preserve your church and make it grow.[2]

Destroy the devil's work;
destroy every force which revolts against you
and every conspiracy against your holy Word.[3]

Do this until your kingdom fully comes,
    when you will be
        all in all.[4]

[1] Ps. 119:5, 105; 143:10; Matt. 6:33
[2] Ps. 122:6-9; Matt. 16:18; Acts 2:42-47
[3] Rom. 16:20; 1 John 3:8
[4] Rom. 8:22-23; 1 Cor. 15:28; Rev. 22:17, 20

LORD'S DAY 49

124 Q. What does the third petition mean?

A. "Your will be done, on earth as it is in heaven" means:

Help us and all people
    to reject our own wills
    and to obey your will without any back talk.
    Your will alone is good.[1]

Help us one and all to carry out the work we are called to,[2]
    as willingly and faithfully as the angels in heaven.[3]

[1] Matt. 7:21; 16:24-26; Luke 22:42; Rom. 12:1-2; Tit. 2:11-12
[2] 1 Cor. 7:17-24; Eph. 6:5-9
[3] Ps. 103:20-21

LORD'S DAY 50

125 Q. What does the fourth petition mean?

   A. "Give us this day our daily bread" means:

> Do take care of all our physical needs[1]
> so that we come to know
>   that you are the only source of everything good,[2]
>   and that neither our work and worry
>   nor your gifts
>   can do us any good without your blessing.[3]

> And so help us to give up our trust in creatures
> and trust in you alone.[4]

[1] Ps. 104:27-30; 145:15-16; Matt. 6:25-34
[2] Acts 14:17; 17:25; James 1:17
[3] Deut. 8:3; Ps. 37:16; 127:1-2; 1 Cor. 15:58
[4] Ps. 55:22; 62; 146; Jer. 17:5-8; Heb. 13:5-6

LORD'S DAY 51

126 Q. What does the fifth petition mean?

   A. "Forgive us our debts,
      as we also have forgiven our debtors" means:

> Because of Christ's blood,
> do not hold against us, poor sinners that we are,
>   any of the sins we do
>   or the evil that constantly clings to us.[1]

> Forgive us just as we are fully determined,
>   as evidence of your grace in us,
> to forgive our neighbors.[2]

[1] Ps. 51:1-7; 143:2; Rom. 8:1; 1 John 2:1-2
[2] Matt. 6:14-15; 18:21-35

LORD'S DAY 52

127 Q. What does the sixth petition mean?

A. "And do not bring us to the time of trial,
but rescue us from the evil one" means:

By ourselves we are too weak
to hold our own even for a moment.[1]
And our sworn enemies—
    the devil,[2] the world,[3] and our own flesh—[4]
never stop attacking us.
And so, Lord,
uphold us and make us strong
    with the strength of your Holy Spirit,
so that we may not go down to defeat
    in this spiritual struggle,[5]
but may firmly resist our enemies
    until we finally win the complete victory.[6]

[1] Ps. 103:14-16; John 15:1-5
[2] 2 Cor. 11:14; Eph. 6:10-13; 1 Pet. 5:8
[3] John 15:18-21
[4] Rom. 7:23; Gal. 5:17
[5] Matt. 10:19-20; 26:41; Mark 13:33; Rom. 5:3-5
[6] 1 Cor. 10:13; 1 Thess. 3:13; 5:23

128 Q. **What does your conclusion to this prayer mean?**

    A.   "For the kingdom
        and the power
        and the glory are yours forever" means:

        We have made all these petitions of you
        because, as our all-powerful king,
            you are both willing and able
            to give us all that is good;[1]
        and because your holy name,
            and not we ourselves,
        should receive all the praise, forever.[2]

[1] Rom. 10:11-13; 2 Pet. 2:9
[2] Ps. 115:1; John 14:13

129 Q. **What does that little word "Amen" express?**

    A.   "Amen" means:

        This shall truly and surely be!

        It is even more sure
            that God listens to my prayer
        than that I really desire
            what I pray for.[1]

[1] Isa. 65:24; 2 Cor. 1:20; 2 Tim. 2:13

NOTES

[1] At the age of fifteen, Ursinus was sent to the University of Wittenberg, the home of Martin Luther, where he studied under the tutelage of Philipp Melanchthon, who was Luther's successor. After an unsuccessful effort at teaching in his hometown of Breaslau, Poland, he then went to Zurich, Switzerland. There he studied under Heinrich Bullinger, who was the successor of the fiery Reformer Ulrich Zwingli, and Peter Martyr Vermigli, who was an Italian Protestant Reformer. For more information see Lyle D. Bierma, *An Introduction to the Heidelberg Catechism: Sources, History, and Theology*, Grand Rapids, Michigan: Baker Books, 2005, pp. 67-70. See also: Karl Barth, trans. Shirley Guthrie, Jr., *The Heidelberg Catechism for Today*, Richmond, Virginia: John Knox Press, 1964, pp. 22-23.

[2] Sidney Mead, *The Lively Experiment: The Shaping of Christianity in America*, Eugene, Oregon: Wipf and Stock Publishers, 2007.

[3] Lyle D. Bierma, Princeton Theological Seminary, Studies in Reformed Theology and History, Number 4, *The Doctrine of the Sacraments on the Heidelberg Catechism: Melancthonian, Calvinist, or Zwinglian?*, Princeton, New Jersey: 1994, p. 41. See also: Bierma, *An Introduction to the Heidelberg Catechism:*

Sources, History, and Theology, Grand Rapids, Michigan: Baker Books, 2005, p. 81.

[4] Karl Barth, trans. Shirley Guthrie, Jr., *The Heidelberg Catechism for Today,* Richmond, Virginia: John Knox Press, 1964, p. 123.

[5] St. Athanasius, *On the Incarnation: De Incarnatione Verbi Dei,* New York: St.Vladimir's Seminary, 1996.

[6] Dante Alighieri, trans. Mark Musa, *The Divine Comedy: Inferno,* New York: Penguin Books, 1971, p. 67.

[7] Karl Barth, trans. Shirley Guthrie, Jr., *The Heidelberg Catechism for Today,* Richmond, Virginia: John Knox Press, 1964, p. 25.

[8] For a further explanation of this thesis, see M. Craig Barnes, *Searching for Home,* Grand Rapids, Michigan: Brazos Press, 2003.

[9] Karl Barth, trans. G.W. Bromiley, *Church Dogmatics: The Doctrine of Reconciliation,* vol. 4.2.60, ed. 22, London: T&T Clark, 2010, p.145.

[10] This material on the grandmothers' tables was published previously in *The Christian Century,* May 20, 2011.

[11] Ann Voskamp, *Selections from One Thousand Gifts: Finding Joy in What Really Matters,* Grand Rapids, Michigan: Zondervan, 2012, p. 31.

[12] C. S. Lewis, *On Stories: And Other Essays on Literature,* New York: Mariner Books, 2002, p. 17.